MUSIC COMPOSITION AND ARRANGING

SAMUEL WALTER

MUSIC COMPOSITION AND ARRANGING

ABINGDON PRESS
NEW YORK • NASHVILLE

MUSIC COMPOSITION AND ARRANGING

Copyright © 1965 by Abingdon Press

Library of Congress Catalog Card Number: 65-10552

SET UP, PRINTED, AND BOUND BY THE
PARTHENON PRESS, AT NASHVILLE,
TENNESSEE, UNITED STATES OF AMERICA

TO LUCIA HERSEY

PREFACE

A person wishing to compose seriously must have a thorough knowledge of the theory of music. Without this knowledge it is impossible to write anything worthwhile. This includes the study of counterpoint and harmony. Before attempting to compose an original piece, one should be able to harmonize correctly a bass or a melody for four voices according to the rules of classical harmony.[1]

Only after one can do this should something original be attempted. One should not begin by trying to write an oratorio or a symphony. Writing a hymn anthem or an organ piece based on a hymn tune is perhaps the easiest way to begin. In the chapters which follow suggestions are made for writing in these two forms.

[1] By classical harmony is meant the system of tonal harmony used in the eighteenth and nineteenth centuries. See "Harmonic Analysis," Willi Apel, *Harvard Dictionary of Music* (Cambridge, Mass.: Harvard University Press, 1944).

The first attempts at composition may be written in classical style and harmony, but before long the composer should try to develop a style more in keeping with today's musical trends. Classical harmony has said about all it can say, as a study of the works of Bach, Mozart, and Brahms shows.

It is my purpose to try to show how a person with training in classical harmony can expand this knowledge and enlarge his musical horizons.

I wish to express my appreciation to Barbara G. Roth for proofreading the manuscript and for helping in matters of clarity and style and to William J. Reynolds for his helpful suggestions in the organization of the material.

Samuel Walter

CONTENTS

Students of harmony are generally taught *classical harmony,* the kind of harmony which was in vogue during the eighteenth and nineteenth centuries. It is based predominantly on the major and their relative, harmonic minor scales. (See Figures 1 and 2.)

FIGURE 1

C Major

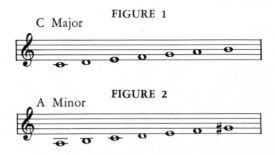

FIGURE 2

A Minor

Above each note in the scale are placed two notes, each the interval of a third apart, to form triads. Each triad has a name and Roman numerals are used to designate the degree of the scale on which the root (lowest note) of the triad appears. The names and degrees are: I, Tonic; II, Supertonic; III, Mediant; IV, Subdominant; V, Dominant; VI, Submediant; VII, Leading Tone. (See Figures 3 and 4.)

CLASSICAL HARMONY

FIGURE 3

C Major Triads

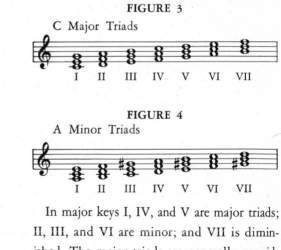

I   II   III   IV   V   VI   VII

FIGURE 4

A Minor Triads

I   II   III   IV   V   VI   VII

In major keys I, IV, and V are major triads; II, III, and VI are minor; and VII is diminished. The major triads are generally considered the most important while the others assume a secondary role.

In minor keys I, IV, and V are considered the most important even though IV and I are minor and only V is major. The remaining triads consist of VI, major; II and VII, diminished; and III, augmented. II, III, and VII can be troublesome and somewhat difficult to handle because each one contains either the sixth or the seventh degree of the scale somewhere in the triad. In A minor these notes are F and G sharp respectively, and together they form the melodic interval of an augmented second. This interval is forbidden melodically and the process of avoiding it may result in awkward voice-leading, or some sort of compromise.

In addition to triads, seventh chords are used; these are created by adding a note a third above the fifth of the triad. (See Figures 5 and 6.) There are seven kinds of seventh chords here, each possessing a distinctive color and function because of its particular combination of major and minor thirds.

The two seventh chords most often used and commonly favored are the dominant seventh (found on V in both major and minor) and the diminished seventh (found on VII in minor).

The dominant seventh (that is, the seventh chord built up on the following combination

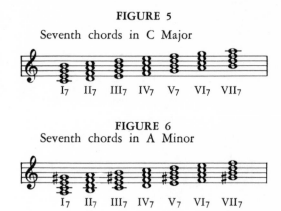

FIGURE 5

Seventh chords in C Major

I_7 II_7 III_7 IV_7 V_7 VI_7 VII_7

FIGURE 6

Seventh chords in A Minor

I_7 II_7 III_7 IV_7 V_7 VI_7 VII_7

of thirds: major, minor, and minor) is not confined to V, the fifth degree of the scale. It may be used on any degree of the scale. It generally resolves to the chord whose root is a fifth below it. This dominant seventh is called *neighbor dominant* (or dominant of tonic, dominant of supertonic, dominant of dominant, et cetera). The hymn tune "Lancashire" works the neighbor dominant to death, as the following excerpt (Figure 7) clearly shows.

The diminished seventh may be used quite freely almost anywhere, and it is a favorite, if rather obvious-sounding, modulatory chord.

To sum up, traditional harmony makes heavy use of I, IV, V, dominant seventh, and diminished seventh chords and tends to neglect the other triads and seventh chords.

This may be an overstatement, certainly if

FIGURE 7

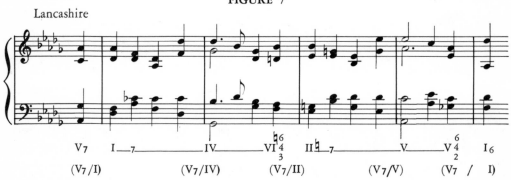

Lancashire

one considers the works of the masters. This book is written chiefly for church musicians, however, and a perusal of nineteenth-century hymns will reveal the paucity of harmonic material used and the lack of variety compared to what is available. The tune "Lancashire," mentioned above, contains only major triads and dominant seventh chords.

This was the way church musicians wrote during the nineteenth century, and it is appalling to realize that of the enormous amount of music published in the United States today, only a very small percentage shows any advance beyond what was written a hundred years ago. It is encouraging, however, to find a small group of composers with talent, imagination, and an experimental and contemporary spirit.

Reharmonizing a hymn tune for four voices is an excellent exercise, and everyone interested in composition should practice it until he can do it easily and correctly according to the rules of classical harmony. If he cannot perform this basic harmonic chore he is handicapped from the start. The ability to ac-cumulate a succession of interesting contemporary sounds will not disguise the lack of thorough training in and understanding of the theory of music.

Try harmonizing a hymn tune several different ways. Be sure to have a strong bass part as it is the foundation on which the other parts are built. Try to make the alto and the tenor parts interesting. Do not let them deteriorate into a succession of repeated notes. Some students try to keep tones common to two chords in the same voice. This is not necessary or desirable if a more interesting voice line is possible.

In the middle of a harmonization one may occasionally run into a snag, where voice-leading according to the rules seems impossible. This may occur between chords on adjacent degrees of the scale (as V to VI, IV to V, et cetera). If this is the case, check to see if the outer voices are moving in opposite directions. Many times this will solve the difficulty. Or go back a few chords and reharmonize them.

Throughout the history of music there has been a tendency to accept as consonant certain intervals which had been considered dissonant in a preceding period. The interval of the third was once dissonant. In the past century the intervals of the second and the seventh were dissonant, and certain rules were applied to their use, both in preparing for the dissonance and in its resolution. Today the second and the seventh may be considered consonant. These seconds and sevenths do not need special preparation or resolution. Consecutive seconds and sevenths are permitted.

Until recently Western music has made use of a system of triads and chords built on the interval of the third. Root position triads and seventh chords illustrate this. Now composers sometimes use chords built on fourths. For example, reading up, a four-note chord built on perfect fourths and starting on C would

EXPANDING THE CONCEPTS OF CLASSICAL HARMONY

be: C, F, B flat, and E flat. As soon as the third note, B flat, is used, the intervals of the seventh and, by inversion, the second occur between C and B flat. When the E flat is added the interval of the third appears. Chords built on fourths tend to have a dry sound compared with chords built on thirds.

There is now a tendency to relax the rules about dissonance, its preparation, and its resolution. Composers often jump into and out of dissonance. In classical harmony thirds, sixths, and sometimes fourths were used consecutively. Today consecutive seconds, fourths, and sevenths are freely used—even parallel fifths and octaves, where this is desirable.

After the composer can harmonize a melody correctly in traditional style he should experiment with contemporary sounds. There are several things he can do.

First, he may take a traditional harmonization and alter some of the notes in the alto, tenor, and bass parts by raising or lowering them a half step. Not all such alterations will be acceptable, however. One must be careful to avoid sounds reminiscent of clichés of "Victorian," Romantic music.

I suggest a heavy use of minor triads and secondary seventh chords in major keys and the elimination of the dominant and diminished seventh chords. The minor triads II, III, and VI will be given emphasis if they are placed on the strong beats of the measure with the major ones on the weak beats, or if the minor triads are of longer duration than the major ones. This will give a somber quality to the music, but it will not necessarily sound "sad." [1]

Classical harmony has certain rules about chord progressions. Some are considered undesirable. Contemporary usage makes no such distinctions. Any chord may be followed by any other one.

SEVENTH CHORDS

The use of the seventh chords tends to make the music more complex. There are the aforementioned seven different seventh chords, the differences among them being the result of the distribution of the major and minor intervals of the third. (See Figure 8.)

Each of these seventh chords is found unaltered somewhere in either the major or the harmonic minor scale. These seventh chords may be used on the degree on which they normally occur. But additional color will be gained if each is used as an altered chord and

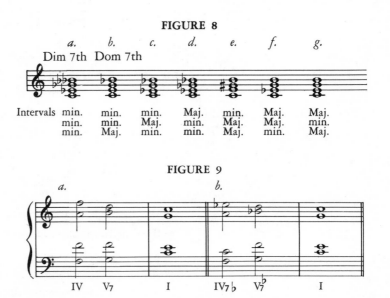

FIGURE 8

FIGURE 9

[1] See Lloyd Pfautsch, "God of Might, We Praise Thy Name," Abingdon Press Music, No. 109, measures 5 to 14 of the accompaniment (p. 79 in this book).

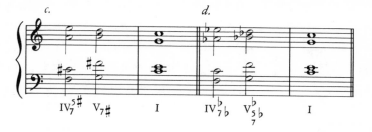

placed anywhere one desires that particular sound. Although the diminished seventh chord generally retains its characteristic sound no matter where it is used, this is not true of the dominant seventh.

Figure 9 contains four examples of the IV-V-I cadential formula illustrating the use of altered seventh chords. The first is the traditional form. The remaining examples use a seventh chord on both IV and V. At *b* in Figure 9 IV$_7$ is the "forbidden" dominant seventh, but it is not characteristic for it to resolve into the form of the seventh which follows it, nor does it sound like the familiar resolution. The V$_7^\flat$ is the same as *c* in Figure 8 and is found unaltered on II, III, and VI in major keys and on IV in harmonic minor ones. The next cadence, *c,* is more dissonant because the two sevenths used are major sevenths, one half step less than an octave. The first, IV$_7^{5\sharp}$, is found on III in harmonic minor scales and the second, V$_7\sharp$, is I$_7$ in major keys. Example *d* is a more somber coloring. The IV$_7^\flat$ is found in major keys on II, III, and VI, and on IV in minor. The V$_7^{5\flat}$ appears on VII in major keys and on II in minor.

Space does not permit giving all the possible combinations using the altered seventh chords (Figure 8) in the progression IV$_7$-V$_7$-I. There is a total of forty-nine combinations. The inquisitive student can, as an exercise,

write out and play other combinations to discover new successions of sound, and to discover which ones he likes or dislikes. Some will sound quite dissonant, others mild. It should be remembered that these altered seventh chords may be introduced, not only in cadences as in Figure 9, but anywhere.

THE NATURAL MINOR SCALE

During the Romantic Period the modes, except major and minor, were neglected. Today there is renewed interest in exploring the possibilities of new modal color. New scales are being constructed with patterns of half steps and whole steps which are different from major and minor.

The preceding material has been directed toward major keys. I should like to discuss now some interesting ways to use the minor mode. Classical harmony generally makes use of the harmonic minor form with the seventh degree of the scale raised one half step. The melodic minor scale, used chiefly for melodic purposes, raises by one half step the sixth and seventh degrees in the ascending form and is unaltered descending. The melodic minor need not concern us here because the descending form is the same as the natural or primitive minor and the ascending form will be discussed later in connection with the formation of new scales.

FIGURE 10

Natural Minor

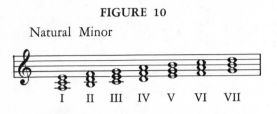

I   II   III   IV   V   VI   VII

The natural minor scale (Figure 10), sometimes called the Aeolian mode, though not a new scale, is generally neglected by classical harmony. With some experimentation, however, the composer may find new combinations of sound with which he is unfamiliar. This scale contains no augmented intervals, thus making possible easier and more logical voice-leading.

The three principal triads, I, IV, and V, are all minor; III, VI, and VII are major; and II is diminished. The notes in the natural scale of A minor are the same as those in C major, but in A minor each note has a different function from its counterpart. C major's tonic is C; the tonic triad is C major. The tonic note of A minor is A; the tonic triad is A minor. In C major the three principal triads, I, IV, and V, are all major; the remainder are minor or diminished. In the natural minor mode, however, the three principal triads, I, IV, and V, are all minor; the remainder are major or diminished. This change from major to minor on the three principal triads produces a color in minor keys quite different from that in major keys. Still other colors will be found

FIGURE 11

a. Harmonic Minor

IV   V♯   7   I

b. Natural Minor

IV   V   7   I

c.

IV   VII   7   I

d.

IV   VII   7♯   I♯

e. in Major

IV   VII   7   I

later on when we discuss other modes and develop new scales.

Further variety of color can be obtained by the use of seventh chords, both unaltered and altered. The familiar harmonic minor cadence, IV-V$_7$-I, is shown at *a* in Figure 11. Note the change of color at *b,* the natural minor form with a natural G. In the natural minor mode the subtonic, VII, may be substituted for the usual dominant, V, with good effect, especially in cadences. I use the word "subtonic" to designate the triad a whole step below the tonic. The term, leading tone, will be used when VII is a *half step* below the tonic tone.

At *c* in Figure 11 the subtonic is used. Furthermore, the seventh chord is a dominant seventh, but the effect is quite different from that of *a* in Figure 9. The dominant seventh in the example in minor (*c,* Figure 11) resolves to the triad one whole step above instead of the usual fifth below the triad (*a,* Figure 9).

The example *d* in Figure 11 is the same as *c* except that the seventh chord on V is altered (F is raised to F sharp) and the final triad, A, is inflected to major. These alterations do not affect the tonality, they merely give additional brightness to the cadence. The altered sevenths may be used in the natural minor mode in the same way as was suggested for their use in major.

The subtonic as an altered chord can be used effectively at cadences and elsewhere in major in place of the dominant (*e,* Figure 11).

It is suggested that the student try using the foregoing material by harmonizing some melodies.

OTHER MODES

The natural minor mode is sometimes called the Aeolian mode and was discussed after the familiar major because of its close connection with the traditional harmonic minor form. For centuries and up to the present time the church had made use of eight modes not including major and minor. Four of these modes are called "authentic," the remainder are called "plagal," and each plagal mode is related to one of the authentic modes. We will examine the four authentic modes and try to discover interesting ways to harmonize them.

In the following study each mode will be placed on the staff in the position requiring no accidentals. If played, only the white keys are used. This is done to show the relationship of each mode to C major.

The harmonization of the modes has received scant attention in classical harmony texts. In *Modern Harmony in Its Theory and Practice,* by Arthur Foote and Walter R. Spalding, which is the text many of us have used, the subject is summarized:

As they do not lend themselves to treatment according to our modern harmonic system, they [the modes] can be appropriately harmonized best by the use of triads, with occasional chords of the 6th (i.e. without chords of the 7th), and do not permit our authentic cadence. The effect produced by them is to our ears something unique; it is undoubtedly because of the refreshing contrast thus obtained that composers are now inclined to return occasionally to their use.[2]

---

[2] Arthur P. Schmidt, 1905, p. 249.

FIGURE 12

Dorian Mode

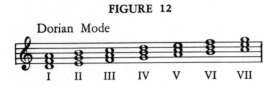

I   II   III   IV   V   VI   VII

Since the writing of this quotation at the turn of the century composers have increasingly returned to the use of the modes, particularly for church music.

Traditionally the modes were harmonized by the use of triads in root position or the first inversion. Seventh chords and second inversions were not used, nor were the diminished triads. Today we need not restrict ourselves to the above rules. Seventh chords of all kinds can be used. The ones which occur unaltered within the mode will help preserve the unique flavor of that mode.

The Dorian mode (Figure 12) is rather somber in color, somewhat like the natural minor scale. Both I and V are minor, and IV is major, showing us a new combination of the principal triads. With this and the following modes I shall illustrate cadences showing the characteristic sounds of the various modes.

The first cadence of Figure 13 is VI-V$_{-7}$-I. Play it and compare the sound of it with that of *b* in Figure 11. Notice the slightly different color inflection between them. At *b* in Figure 13 the progression IV-VII$_{-7}$-I is used. It seems to me that the penultimate VII gives better modal color to the cadence, and one which is more characteristic of the mode than does V.

Strict organum, which is the earliest example of harmony and which consisted chiefly of progressions of fourths and fifths, did permit the interval of the third as the penultimate interval before the final unison. If the lower note is considered the root, the pro-

FIGURE 13

IV   V   7   I   IV   VII   7   I

FIGURE 14

gression is VII-I. It may be because of the frequent use of this cadence (third going to a unison) in early two-part modal music that the modern four-part harmonizations using VII-I in cadences sound more typically modal than ones using V-I. Figure 14 shows a four-teenth century German carol in the Dorian mode.

The Phrygian mode is from E to E. The triads for the various degrees are shown in Figure 15. The dominant, V, falls on B, and the triad is diminished. The interval B to F, the tritone or diminished fifth, was avoided traditionally, and in this mode the dominant note is shifted to VI or C.

Example *a* in Figure 16 is a cadence using VI instead of V, and *b* is the IV-VII₇-I progression. However, *c* sounds more like a typical Phrygian cadence. The degrees above and below the final (II and VII) are used before I.

FIGURE 15

Phrygian Mode

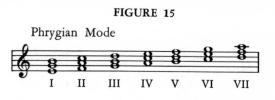

This is the only mode with only a half step between the first and second degrees of the scale; the others are a whole step apart. Therefore, the Phrygian mode has a color quite distinctive from the others. A typical Phrygian color is found in the theme from Brahms' *Symphony in E minor* (Figure 17).

The Lydian mode (Figure 18) is like the major except that the fourth degree is a half step higher than the major. Traditionally the fourth degree of the Lydian mode was often lowered a half step, creating a scale identical to the major. IV was lowered by one half step (B to B flat) whenever there was a strong

FIGURE 16

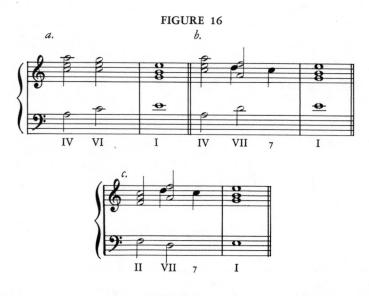

FIGURE 17

FIGURE 18

Lydian Mode

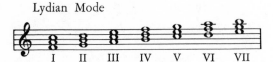

I II III IV V VI VII

FIGURE 19

II VII 7 I

tritone influence between I and IV (F and B). The typical Lydian color, however, is largely a result of the B natural in context with an F major tonic. Because the tritone is freely used today, the Lydian color will be emphasized if the notes F and B are present in adjacent chords. The subdominant is a diminished triad and is therefore unsuitable as a true subdominant. The best cadence to illustrate

The Mixolydian mode (Figure 21) sounds very much like major, and the final cadence often sounds like a half cadence on the dominant of major. This is somewhat characteristic of this mode, however. This mode is like major except that the VII of Mixolydian is

FIGURE 20

Tan - tum er - go Sa - cra - men - tum

Lydian color is the one which uses the degree above and the degree below the final: II-VII-7-I. (See Figure 19.) This is the same progression as was used for the Phrygian cadence at *c* in Figure 16. The Lydian color is shown in the excerpt from the plainchant hymn *Tantum ergo* (Figure 20).

one half step lower than VII of major. The two examples of Mixolydian cadences in Figure 22 sound, even to my ear, which is used to modal sounds, like unfinished cadences in C major, as though the C major triad should follow the G. Figure 23 shows a harmonization of a Mixolydian melody, taken from the Episcopal *Hymnal, 1940,* No. 658.

The composer wishing to experiment in the modes may prefer to concentrate on the Dorian, Phrygian, and Aeolian (natural minor). It is easier to capture the distinctive

FIGURE 21

Mixolydian Mode

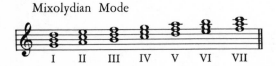

I II III IV V VI VII

FIGURE 22

a.   b.

IV V 7 I   IV VII 7 I

FIGURE 23

My soul doth mag - ni - fy the Lord,*

and my spi - rit hath rejoiced in God my Sa - viour.

sounds of these modes than those of the Lydian and Mixolydian.

The cadence in major (at *e* in Figure 11) uses the subtonic in the progression IV-VII$_7$-I. This subtonic triad is B flat major, a triad not found in C major. It is VII with a flat (lowered) root. Any of the degrees of the scale may be altered and any of the triads may be changed from major to minor and from minor to major at will. Diminished triads may be made minor or major.

Figure 24 is a cadence of five triads IV-V-VI-VII-I. VI and VII are lowered and the

FIGURE 24

IV   V   VI   VII   I

fifth of the former is also lowered. Such a succession of major triads gives a bright color. If VI and VII are consistently lowered in C major, we have virtually a new scale.

NEW SCALES

Lucia Hersey, who taught theory at the same time I taught organ and courses in church music at Boston University, was the first person to show me how traditional harmonic concepts could be enlarged to include contemporary practices. The material which follows is basically hers, and I hope to give a clear and true picture of what she taught me.

After working for some time in the traditional idiom Professor Hersey suggested that by raising or lowering a degree tone by a half

FIGURE 25

step in one voice and retaining the tone un-altered in another the element of dissonance would be added. Figure 25 illustrates this: *a* contains no alterations; *b* has a G sharp in the melody. The G sharp has a startling, piquant effect. This method of arbitrary dissonance can very easily sound contrived, however. It is more logical to create new scales which contain inherent dissonance.

FIGURE 26

For example, the scale B to B (Figure 26) is really the Locrian mode, not a new scale, but rather a theoretical mode and one certainly not widely used. The difficulty of using this mode as it now stands for harmonic writing lies in the fact that the tonic triad, I, is diminished—B, D, and F, a very poor triad for the final one of a composition. If, however, a major or a minor triad is built above each of the degree tones in the scale new harmonic progressions become available.

FIGURE 27

I   II   III   IV   V   VI   VII

Figure 27 shows a minor triad on I with all the remaining degrees major. This scale tends to be very bright sounding because of the many major triads, but resolves to a strange somberness on the final, I.

FIGURE 28

IV   V 7   I

Figure 28 is the familiar IV-V^{-7}-I cadence, but this one has a fresh different sound. Figure 27 is the "harmonic" form of the scale. If all the notes that appear in the harmonic form are arranged in order we have the "melodic" form of the scale (Figure 29). The harmonic form is the foundation for the basic harmonies, and the melodic form is freely used melodically in all voices and to create dissonance. Figure 30 is an easy, obvious example to show this. The lower staff contains a simple harmonic progression with the melody exploiting dissonance on the staff above it.

Any succession of notes may be used as the basis for a new scale, and the number of notes need not be confined to the traditional seven. William Wallace of Rutgers University is interested in the creation of new scales, and he has used some of them as the basis for his compositions.

Two of Dr. Wallace's scales are found in Figure 31. Both of these scales contain eight different notes instead of the usual seven. The first scale is composed of several overlapping but identical tetrachords, if enharmonic changes in spelling are used. The second scale is composed of two disjunctive tetra-

FIGURE 29

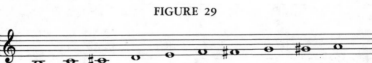

FIGURE 30

FIGURE 31

Used by permission of William Wallace.

chords, and each tetrachord is the same; that is, each is composed of the same intervals. These tetrachords (*b,* Figure 31) are unusual because of the augmented second interval between the second and the third notes. There are, therefore, two augmented intervals in the complete scale.

Dr. Wallace elaborated further on his new scales and how they may be used in composition:

It is interesting to observe that the very *symmetricality* of these two scales disorients the ear and automatically leads to a weaker sense of tonality than that afforded by the traditional diatonic scales. In the latter the irregular distribution of the half steps among the whole steps makes it difficult for the ear to mistake any degree of the scale for any other; in the scales under consideration, however, such "mistakes" are inevitable, there being degrees other than the tonic above which lie, without chromatic alteration, eight-note scales identical in structure to that ly-

ing above the tonic. Indeed, such scale degrees can sound as "tonic" as the tonic itself.

Neither scale is particularly well adapted for use in a way resembling traditional harmonic functionalism. Examination will reveal a dearth of major and minor triads for degrees of the scale other than the tonic. Furthermore, the presence of an extra scale-degree in both cases strips the chords of their traditional meanings. "V," for example, is disrupted into the position of an augmented fourth above the tonic, with three chords above it instead of the usual two, and loses its dominant flavor in consequence.

When the scales are used harmonically, the composer [Dr. Wallace] sees no particular reason for a consistent procedure of building them up on thirds and has made no attempt in this direction, although such is possible. Rather, he has availed himself of whatever interval-combinations have been suggested by the expressive purpose of the moment. There actually exists a wide variety of possible sounds to choose from without chromatic alteration, and personal experimentation

25

must be the source of their discovery. The second scale will be found to be especially intriguing in its harmonic possibilities.

It is possible, of course, to use either scale as a basis for melody as well as harmony, or for melody and harmony simultaneously. With regard to the second scale, there lies an obvious danger that the consistent presence of the augmented seconds will become tiresome melodically. However, there is clearly no need for a constant adherence to either scale.

Shifting from one of the scales to another identical in structure but built from another of the twelve tones is a valuable means of increasing variety and scope. It is best in so doing to avoid effecting a shift to a scale whose notes lie, without chromatic alteration, wholly on the original scale, as this gives insufficient sense of change. One can, of course, "modulate" also by shifting to a scale different in structure.

It should be noted that, by treating different degrees of these scales as tonics, different "modes" are available. For example, treating *D* in the first scale as tonic yields a different effect from C. However, it is obvious that not all of the "modes" will actually be different in structure.

CHORDS BUILT ON FOURTHS

Thus far we have discussed music in which the chords have been built up chiefly on the interval of the third. Chords may be built up on any interval. Chords built up on fourths are often seen but it seems to me that they are of limited use over extended periods of composition. The texture is somewhat dry.

Figure 32 shows examples of three-, four-, and five-note chords built on fourths. As soon as the fourth note is added (*b*) the interval of

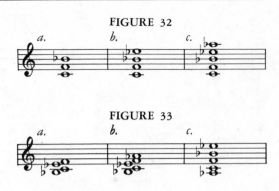

FIGURE 32

FIGURE 33

the third appears between C and E flat and with the fifth note added (*c*) the triad, F, A flat, C, appears. Variants of chords built on fourths are given in Figure 33. The next step is to create chords from any combination of tones.

TWELVE-TONE SCALES

If one pursues the subject of contemporary music to its logical conclusion it leads quite naturally to the admitting of all the tones within the octave, twelve of them, into musical composition. In this type of writing there is generally an attempt made to give equal emphasis to each of the twelve tones and to negate any semblance of a tonal center. Very little church music has been written in this idiom. Courageous composers should experiment in the twelve-tone system.

I believe that some modification of the above (equal emphasis to each of the twelve tones and the negation of a tonal center) can be made with acceptable results; namely, the inclusion of a tonal center. It need not be a triad; it may be a single note which gives a point of reference and around which the other notes revolve. This tonal center may be well defined or it may be vague.

CONCLUSION

Today composers do not necessarily use only one type of writing within a given composition. The texture may vary from being very complex and opaque to very simple and transparent. Chords composed of only fourths, fifths, and octaves may be used wherever this texture is desired.

In general, it seems that composers tend to create the more complex combinations of tone within the phrase and to use thinner combinations at the cadences. If the final chord is a seventh chord, it may be preceded by complex chords built on fourths. In classical harmony seventh chords often preceded the final triad. Triadal writing may lead into a final unison or a perfect fifth.

Further suggestions will be made in the chapters which follow and pieces by contemporary composers will be analyzed.

Now, take a melody and harmonize it in a contemporary idiom, keeping the individual voice parts interesting and logical, avoiding parallel fifths and octaves particularly in the outer voices, and, as much as is practical, making the bass part move in contrary motion to the melody. The harmonization should be played on the piano so that the composer can be sure he has written the sounds he wants.

One of the most effective kinds of writing is that which introduces the various phrases of the hymn tune by polyphonic entrances for all the voices and which is imitative of the hymn tune. Some tunes lend themselves more easily than others. A strong melody with motion and skips is generally better than a weak melody with many scale lines and repeated notes.

As an exercise, try writing a trio: one voice for the right hand, one voice for the left hand, and one for the pedals. Choose a strong melody. Decide which voice will present the melody in its entirety; it may be any one of the three. Start by writing one measure of the first phrase of the tune in an accompanimental voice. Begin the second accompanimental voice after one measure (other units, such as a half measure, or two measures may work better) and write in the same number of melody notes as appear in the first measure of the first voice. The second voice may start on any pitch. The octave and the fifth are frequently

WRITING FOR ORGAN

used. Next continue the first voice. Whether the hymn-tune melody should still be used or not will depend on the nature of the tune and on the composer's harmonic inclinations. Continuation of strict canonic imitation after the second voice has started can produce sharp dissonances which may be incompatible with the composer's wishes. When this occurs alteration of the offending notes by a half step or a whole step often makes the harmony more palatable. It is important for the sounds to be agreeable to the composer's ear! If continuing the strict canonic imitation produces excessive dissonance, the imitation may be dropped in favor of a freely composed voice.

Sometime after the second voice has started the melody itself in the third voice, the one which will take the melody in its original form and in its entirety, will enter. Sometimes interest is gained by writing the melody in augmentation; that is, each note in the melody will be twice (or other multiple) as long as the thematic entrances of the two accompanimental voices at the beginning of the piece.

Write down one phrase of the melody and then add the two accompanimental voices. Try to make these two voices interesting; they should not deteriorate into mere chordal accompaniment for the melody.

At the conclusion of the phrase of the melody the accompanimental voices will drop out one by one, and after a brief rest resume by introducing the next phrase. This entrance may begin on the final note of the melody or after it. In order to maintain a rhythmic continuity, care should be taken not to end phrases in all three voices at the same time. They should dovetail with one another.

Continue the composition in the manner outlined above until the entire melody has been used. Then a few measures of cadential material should give a sense of completeness to the piece. This material may be derived from the melody. Sometimes the final phrase can be repeated. The final note of the melody may be held to the end or not, as the composer wishes.

Pieces may be written for more than three voices, but the texture should be kept clear and transparent. Additional notes, merely to fill out the chords, should be avoided.

The prelude on the tune "O Gott, du frommer Gott" [1] is a simple trio with thematic material in all the voices. The middle voice begins the melody. The lowest voice starts the same melody after four beats, one octave lower. The top voice enters after three beats, in a higher octave, and presents the melody in augmentation. The two lower voices complete the first phrase of the melody before using composed free material which is needed to accompany the longer notes of the top voice. On the last note of the phrase in the top voice, the middle voice stops for two beats before beginning the second phrase. Again, after one measure, and one octave lower, the lowest voice takes the same melody and is followed after three beats by the augmented melody in the top voice. The remainder of the prelude is treated consistently in the same manner: The middle voice enters on the last note of the melody in the top voice; the lowest voice enters one measure later, one octave below the middle voice, and uses the same thematic material; and the top voice enters after three beats, one octave above the middle voice, and takes the phrase in augmentation.

There is only one exception to this exact imitation. On the fourth beat of measure 34 and the first beat of measure 35 the lowest voice does not continue the strict imitation. The same direction of the melody is maintained but the intervals are different. Why did I not rigidly adhere to strict imitation at this point? It is difficult to say. Possibly, because I did not feel like it and wanted the particular sounds which the change made possible.

Note the regularity with which each phrase of the lowest voice ends—a downward scale

[1] Samuel Walter, *Nine Compositions for Organ* (Nashville: Abingdon Press, 1965).

passage of at least five notes. The end of the piece is extended by introducing this five-note motif into the middle voice before the final cadence.

Some melodies do not adapt themselves as readily to polyphonic imitation as do others. Sometimes it might not be wise to maintain the same distance (meter and interval) in the imitations. In fact, the imitation need not be strict at all, but may be free. Deviations from strict imitation should be made wherever necessary to bring the harmonies into agreement with the composer's desires. Strict imitation can at times produce the wildest sounds, sounds which the composer does not like. It then becomes necessary to modify some of the notes. Changes should be made to conform with the composer's wishes. It is a somewhat arbitrary procedure to continue strict imitation merely for its own sake.

THE USE OF CANON

Some tunes can be used as a canon. The canonic voice may follow the melody at any pitch or time interval. I have the impression that many times the canonic voice is not recognized as such, particularly when pitch intervals other than the octave are used.

Bach has left us several examples of canonic writing. In his *Orgelbüchlein* the chorale is treated as a canon in the following preludes: "Gott, durch deine Güte," one measure and one octave; "In dulci jubilo," double canon at the octave and one measure's distance; "O Lamm Gottes, unschuldig," canon at the fifth

and two beats; "Christe, du Lamm Gottes," the accompaniment begins canonically in three voices, and at measure 4 the melody begins in the tenor register and is followed one measure later by the soprano, an example of canon at the twelfth; "Christus, der uns selig macht," canon at the octave and two beats; "Hilf Gott, dass mir's gelinge," canon at the fifth and two beats; "Erschienen ist der herrliche Tag," canon at the octave and one measure; and "Liebster Jesu, wir sind hier," canon at the fifth and two beats.

The prelude on "Kirken den er et" [2] is polyphonically written with the melody treated in strict canon at the octave. The piece begins with three accompanimental voices, with each in turn taking the first phrase of the melody. The first voice begins in the tenor register, the second voice a sixth above the first, and the third voice a seventh above the second voice. A rest follows the last note of the melody phrase, and the lowest voice takes the second phrase of the melody with the other two voices adding simple harmony. At measure 8 the lowest accompanimental voice is just completing the second phrase, the top voice finishes and will drop out, and the melody proper is heard on the pedals. Two measures later and one octave above, the canonic voice enters in strict imitation. Both the rhythm and the intervals are exact. While the canon is being heard two accompanimental voices supply simple harmony. Two phrases of the melody are heard before there is a return of the imitation supplied by the accompanimental voices, at which time the first part is repeated.

Continuing along in the piece, there fol-

[2] *Ibid.*

lows an interlude similar to the beginning. This time the second voice begins a third above the first, and the third voice begins a fifth above the second. The lowest voice again introduces a second new phrase as it did at the beginning, but this time several changes are made in the actual notes of the phrase of the melody which will be heard a little later in canon. This was done to prepare the harmony for the next pedal entrance of the melody proper. The top accompanimental voice consistently drops out before the canon begins. The pedal enters and again the canonic voice imitates it strictly at two measures and one octave distance. This time the remainder of the melody (three phrases) is used with no interspersed episodic material. The final phrase makes use of thematic material derived from the first and the last phrases of the melody.

Sometimes a greater sense of unity can be given to a piece by this simple means: Use at least fragments of introductory thematic material at or near the end of the piece. In this instance, at measure 53 the first and second accompanimental voices take the first phrase of the melody (as they did in measures 1 to 4), the third voice takes the last phrase of the melody at measure 55.

Adhering to strict imitation for the greater part of the time produces the rather angular, somewhat dry harmonies, which I feel are compatible with the melody.

Some tunes lend themselves better than others to canonic imitation. Some, though not effective at the octave, can be used at other intervals.

The inquisitive student should study the canon as used by both the old masters and modern ones, such as Dr. Seth Bingham.

REHARMONIZATION OF MELODIES

Another type of writing for the organ is a homophonic reharmonization of the melody. This may be a simple chordal setting, note against note like many harmonizations in the hymnal, or it may be more elaborate, with passing notes in the lower voices, like a Bach chorale harmonization.

A hymn tune, chorale, plainchant, or folk melody may be harmonized in several different musical styles. It should be written in the best taste possible. Writing in a late nineteenth-century style, with a heavy use of chromaticism, altered notes, diminished sevenths, dominant sevenths, and neighbor dominants, should be avoided. This style is particularly ill suited for the harmonization of chorale and plainchant tunes. Both the chorale and plainchant have a character of their own which is incompatible with lush Romantic color.

If the composer can do it, I urge that he try writing in a contemporary idiom. When done with care and taste, no violation of the integrity of the tune need occur. Composers throughout the history of music have written in a style which was contemporary in their own day even when they used pre-existing melodies. Bach used chorale melodies, some of which were about two centuries old in his day, but he harmonized them in his own style.

Plainchant melodies may be harmonized in an archaic-contemporary style. The use of open fourths and fifths without thirds and sixths may be used in contrast to more complex chords. If triads are used traditional modal progressions as well as new modal colors are possible.

The prelude "Eucharistic Hymn"[3] is composed simply of two harmonized versions of the tune with episodic material from the tune at the beginning, middle, and end.

The first four notes of the melody are used as a motif twice, followed by most of the last phrase of the melody, which leads into a four-part harmonization of the melody at measure 8.

The first harmonization, measures 8 to 23, opens with a pedal-point on E flat which continues for almost five measures, and thereafter the pedal moves mostly stepwise with a few skips. From measures 18 to 23 the pedal moves chiefly in dotted whole notes. The pedal part was written without too much motion to give a sense of quietness which the hymn suggests. The inner two voices move in what I considered to be interesting lines. There are many intervals of seconds and sevenths, sometimes used successively. This use of consecutive seconds and sevenths gives a somewhat contemporary color. The subtonic note, D flat, the note a whole tone below the tonic, and chords with that note in them are used throughout the piece to give color.

Following the harmonization of the melody, at measure 24, the opening four-note motif appears twice. Then, without a modulation, the tune is harmonized again, in four parts, in the key of A flat. No modulation is needed because of the constant use of the subtonic chord (D flat major) up to this point. Using the D flat chord anticipates the key of A flat.

The second harmonization is for manuals alone. At measure 28, the lowest voice takes a pedal-point on E flat for four measures. This is the same note used in measures 8 to 12, but this time it is the dominant of A flat rather than the tonic of E flat. This dominant resolves to the tonic A flat at measure 32. The subtonic, G flat, used twice in measures 33 and 34, suggests the color of the first harmonization. Otherwise the G natural is used. The inner voices move but there are many long notes which help to maintain the quiet calm of the piece.

At measures 42 to 44, the logical dominant-to-tonic progression in A flat is avoided. This was done, with the use of the D natural and the pedal note, E flat, to bring the tonality back to E flat.

The end of the piece is somewhat like the beginning. The four-note motif is used twice, and then comes the final phrase of the melody, but this time the repetition of the four-note motif appears an octave and a whole step above the first statement. This is a coloristic device. The last phrase (four measures in the hymn tune) is expanded into eight measures to bring the piece to a quiet conclusion.

The prelude "Hyfrydol"[4] is a study in contemporary sounds. Fanfares at the beginning (four measures), middle (six measures), and end (ten measures) alternate with the two harmonized versions of the hymn tune. The fanfares are simply a succession of major and minor chords, some related to F major, the key of the piece, and some not. The succession of major chords in the first three measures is: C, B flat, C, A flat, F, and A. The

[3] *Ibid.*

[4] *Ibid.*

fourth measure contains the major chords E, D, and E flat in the right hand and the minor chords C sharp, B, and C in the left hand. This produces a series of secondary seventh chords between the hands.

In the harmonized version of the melody which follows there is a heavy use of chords containing two, three, or four intervals of the fourth, and chords containing second and seventh intervals. Examples of the former appear in measures 5, 9, 10, 11, 13, and 18. Measures 21 and 22 contain a series of three-note chords built on fourths, which is repeated a step lower in measures 23 and 24. An example of a series of parallel sevenths is shown in the two lowest voices in measures 17 and 18. At measure 26 altered chords with tones not in the key of F major are used. The final note of the melody is harmonized with a four-note chord built on fourths, which in root position would read upward: D, G, C, and F.

The interlude which follows contains major, minor, and seventh chords, similar to the introduction but using other chords.

The second harmonization of the melody is not as "dry" sounding as the first because it contains more traditional triads and seventh chords than the first. For variety, from measure 51 to 57, the three lowest voices take a duple meter against the triple meter of the melody. Beginning with measure 58 there is a series of cadences in other keys: Measure 59, A flat; 60, F minor; 61, G flat; 62, E flat minor; 63, D minor; and 66, G minor. The final phrase, beginning at measure 71, is composed mostly of simple major triads, in the following order: A flat, C dominant seventh, F minor, C minor, D, C, B flat, A, D minor, E flat, and F.

The final fanfare of ten measures emphasizes the F chord, the tonic of the tonality of the piece. In fact, the F chord appears somewhere in each of the last ten measures.

THE MELODY IN LOWER VOICES

The melody may be used in other voices than the top one. "Eucharistic Hymn" and "Hyfrydol" are harmonized with the melody in the top voice. Sometimes it may be desirable to place the melody in the alto, tenor, or bass register. The supporting voices may be polyphonic, harmonic, or a combination of both.

If the melody is to appear in the bass register, care should be taken to make sure that objectionable chord inversions and progressions are avoided. For example, if one were to reharmonize the tune "St. Anne" in a tradi-

FIGURE 34

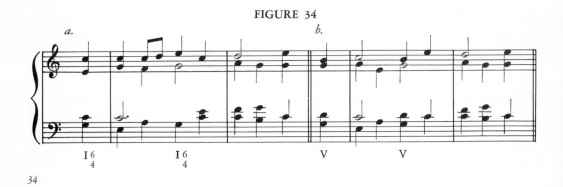

tional manner with the melody in the bass, the first and fourth notes, G (when the tune is in the key of C), should not be harmonized on the C chord. If the C chord is used the second inversion ($^6_4$), which is used chiefly at cadences or in diatonic scale-line passages, would be the opening chord of the piece. Figure 34 *a* illustrates this. At *b* the alternate harmonization avoids the second inversion by substituting chords in root position.

"Rendez à Dieu"[5] is a simple setting of the tune in the tenor register, with two introductory phrases derived from the melody and two at the conclusion. The piece opens with three voices, entering polyphonically, imitating the melody, though the middle voice is not strict imitation. The lowest voice begins the melody but abandons it after the fourth note. The second voice enters after one measure, a sixth above the first voice, and the top voice takes the melody of the first phrase of the tune after one measure and a third above the middle voice. All three voices end the phrase together. At measure 6 all the voices enter as they did at the beginning, but a third lower. The first four measures are repeated with only one note changed, and at measure 10 the voices return to the tonality of G.

The second phrase leads into a simple harmonization of the tune, which appears in the tenor register. The pedals contain the bass part, and the right hand fills out the harmony. The melody repeats its first two phrases, but on the repeat the voice leading and the harmony are different. At the conclusion of the melody the last two phrases of the melody are repeated by the accompanimental

voices, with the melody in the top voice. The first of these two phrases, however, is in B minor and the last one is in G, the tonality of the piece. The shift to B minor gives a quality of freshness to the tonality of the final phrase.

The form of the prelude "Herzliebster Jesu"[6] is simply two harmonized versions of the melody, with a short introduction, an interlude, and an extended cadence at the end. The introduction is composed of two phrases; the first is four measures long, the second is three measures long and overlaps the melody by one measure. The top voice of the first phrase is derived from the melody. A coloristic device, successions of perfect fifths for the left hand, is used as the bass throughout the piece except in the second harmonization of the melody. This device and the generally somber harmonies were used to give appropriate color to this Lenten chorale.

In the first harmonization the melody is given to the pedals at 4' pitch (if this is possible on the particular organ on which it is played), thus placing the melody in the treble register. On organs without available 4' pitch, or with a twenty-five note pedal board, the melody will sound in a lower register. The succession of perfect fifths is continued in the left hand with the right hand taking three-note chords.

The interlude overlaps the melody by beginning on the last note of the latter and is a modification of the introduction. There are two phrases, each three measures long. The second phrase does not overlap the melody this time, but ends with a two-beat rest.

[5] *Ibid.*

[6] *Ibid.*

A four-part harmonization of the melody with the bass part on the pedals follows. The final note of the melody is held for six measures while the other voices make use of material somewhat like the introduction and bring the piece to its conclusion.

Several technical devices were used to give a dark color to the piece. The use of the successive perfect fifths in the left hand has been mentioned. Many chords have no third but consist only of fourths, and fifths, and octaves.

Some chords contain, in addition to these intervals, seconds and sevenths. Secondary seventh chords are frequently used. Simple triads are used to contrast both the open sounding chords with no thirds and the more complex sounding seventh chords.

EMBELLISHED MELODY

Another type of writing is that in which the melody itself is changed. It may be very simply embellished by the addition of a few passing notes or it may be more elaborate with many added notes. In fact, the result may sound like a new melody, and the original may be lost. For example, the Brahms organ chorale prelude "Es ist ein' Ros' entsprungen," from opus 122, is based on the familiar "Lo, how a rose e'er blooming," but the melody is lost in the Brahms setting. (See Figure 35.)

Another example (Figure 36), from Bach's *Orgelbüchlein*, shows a highly embellished mel-

FIGURE 35

Melody of "Es ist ein' Ros' entsprungen"

Brahm's version

FIGURE 36

Melody of "O Mensch, bewein' dein' Sünde gross"

Bach's version

FIGURE 37

Melody of "Liebster Jesu"

ody in "O Mensch, bewein' dein' Sünde gross."

Simple chords are often sufficient accompaniment to the embellished melody.

A study of the embellished melody in the seventeenth and eighteenth century chorale prelude would be worthwhile.

In "Liebster Jesu" [7] the chorale melody is embellished and is accompanied by very simple chords. After two measures of accompanimental chords, the melody begins and is set once.

Two additional measures end the piece. The treatment here used virtually obliterates the original melody. (See Figure 37.) Though all the notes of the original melody are present except one, the rhythm is changed, and many of the melody notes are placed at weak points in the measure. It is not necessary nor always desirable to embellish a melody beyond recognition. The embellishment may consist of a few passing notes with no changes in the basic rhythm.

THE TOCCATA

A brief perusal of toccatas for organ written during the Romantic period and in more recent years shows that many of them are based on a simple pattern of notes or chords that lie well for the hands and can be played rapidly. It is not easy to write interesting toccata patterns, however. Series of chords, arpeggios, or other combinations may be taken by both hands, divided between the hands, or each hand may take its own pattern.

The latter method is used by Charles-Marie Widor in the "Toccata" from his *Fifth Symphony*. The first measure (Figure 38) sets the pattern for the whole piece. The right hand takes arpeggios and the left hand chords. After eight measures for manuals alone, the pedal enters at measure 9 and takes the same melody as the manuals. (See Figure 39.) This

FIGURE 38

Copyright by Edward B. Marks Music Corporation. Used by permission.

[7] *Ibid.*

FIGURE 39

section (A') is altered and expanded into twelve measures. There follows a middle section, still based on the opening pattern, which is a harmonic excursion into other keys. It eventually leads into the next section (A''). (See Figure 40.) A coda and a few chords end the piece. Occasionally the patterns are re-versed, and the right hand arpeggio figure is take by the left hand and the right hand takes the chords. (See Figure 41.) The interesting feature about this toccata is the simplicity of its organization. Perhaps this accounts, at least partly, for its great popularity.

In the "Toccata" from *Suite Gothique* by

FIGURE 40

FIGURE 41

FIGURE 42

Léon Boëllmann two types of patterns are used. The first is started in the first measure (Figure 42) with the right hand taking arpeggios and the left hand simple chords. In measure 3 the pedal enters with a simple melody not derived from the manuals.

This melody ends at measure 20, and a slightly different toccata figure is introduced. (See Figure 43.) Here the left hand takes a simple arpeggio figure, and the right hand has a melody. This leads into a return of the first section transposed from C minor to G minor. Again the second pattern follows the G minor section which in turn leads back to the original key of C minor and a repetition of the first section, exactly as it was stated the first time except that the pedals sometimes double at the octave. Once more the second theme is used and the piece ends with a return of the first melody. The form of the piece is simply A-B-A (transposed) B-A-B-A (fragment). The B sections may be thought of as episodic and modulatory material. Here again the form is extremely simple.

In the *Toccata for Organ* by Eugène Gigout a melody is introduced as part of the toccata

FIGURE 43

FIGURE 44

Copyright by Edward B. Marks Music Corporation. Used by permission.

FIGURE 45

Copyright by Edward B. Marks Music Corporation. Used by permission.

pattern. (See Figure 44.) Later this melody is used on the pedals with a different pattern on the manuals. (See Figure 45.) Still later the same melody is embellished with passing notes, and the manual toccata pattern is changed. (See Figure 46.) There is interesting use made of both the theme and the toccata patterns for episodic material with modulation between the three statements of the theme and in the coda.

In Mulet's toccata "Tu es petra" from *Esquisses Byzantines* two types of writing are used to develop the piece in an interesting manner. (See Figure 47.)

In these examples a toccata pattern of fast notes is used on the manuals. The melody on the pedals generally contains notes of longer value. This type of writing permits the pedal to be heard to best advantage. Toccatas often end with full, longer note-value chords on the manuals. This gives more sound and a more thrilling ending.

The prelude "Slane" [8] is an example of a toccata. The melody, "Slane," is a strong tune with a decidedly "different" color because of the pentatonic scale influence. A pentatonic scale on C is C, D, E, G, and A. The note B (not in this pentatonic scale) appears only

FIGURE 46

Copyright by Edward B. Marks Music Corporation. Used by permission.

[8] *Ibid.*

FIGURE 47

First type of writing

Second type of writing

three times, each time at a weak place in the measure. Except for these three passing notes on B, the melody lies entirely in the pentatonic scale.

Against the melody a toccata figure is set. This figure is composed of a combination of chords built on thirds and chords built on fourths.

A three-note chord built on fourths is given to the right hand while the left hand takes minor and major chords. The B flats, A flats, and E flats are used to give color.

At the conclusion of the melody there is a four-measure interlude which leads into the second statement of the melody, this time in the top voice. The toccata figure is continued though somewhat modified, and the pedals take a bass line. The final note of the melody is extended into four measures. The short

coda of five measures is chordal to give greater volume. The bass line goes down, and the manuals go up to give emphasis to the final tonic chord.

THEME AND VARIATIONS

The form of the theme and variations is obvious. A melody is used in a number of ways. The melody itself may be altered, the accompaniment may be varied, and the textures may be changed. Any of the hymn-tune prelude forms discussed in this chapter may be used as a variation.

The theme itself should be set simply so that it will be recognized when it is used in the variations. An original four-part harmonized version, perhaps in a contemporary idiom, could be used.

Many examples of this form, called also the organ partita, have been written from the seventeenth century to the present time. An interesting example is the organ partita, "Jesu, meine Freude," by Johann Gottfried Walther. The first two measures of four of the first nine partitas and the two measures containing the opening statement of the theme (in the pedal part) of Partita 10 are shown in Figure 48.

FIGURE 48

Jesu, meine Freude
Partita 1.

Partita 4.

Partita 6.

Partita 9.

Partita 10. Measures 11-12 (First pedal entrance)

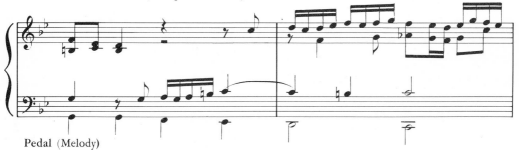

Pedal (Melody)

Partita 1 is a harmonization of the chorale with some passing notes. Upper auxiliary notes embellish the melody in number 4. In number 6 the melody appears in the alto register with chromatic harmonies above and below it. The rhythmic number 9 gives another treatment of the melody. Number 10 is a four-voice fughetta in which the melody appears on the pedals. The fughetta subject is shown in Figure 49.

simple major or minor triads or seventh chords with the third omitted.

Further departure from the original melody is made in variation III. Several notes of the melody are omitted and a contrasting triple meter is used. Measures 5 to 8 are a repetition and a rearrangement of the voices of measures 1 to 4. The melody is first in the top voice (measures 1 to 4) and then in the lowest (measures 5 to 8). From measures 9 to 12 the

FIGURE 49

"God rest you merry"[9] is an example of the theme and variations. The theme is given out in the right hand and is accompanied by a strict canon at the octave and after one beat in the left hand. In the first variation the melody remains unchanged. The left hand consists of rhythmic punctuation produced from chords built on fourths. In variation II the melody, in the left hand, is somewhat modified and is accompanied by staccato chords of

melody is in the top voice. In measure 12 the left hand again takes the melody, which reverts to the top voice in the last phrase. At measure 16 the two lowest voices take a duple meter against the triple meter of the melody. Above a syncopated pedal point, fragments of the melody are used in a syncopated way in variation V. Again fragments of the melody appear in the finale.

[9] *Ibid.*

This chapter will deal chiefly with writing hymn anthems; that is, making an arrangement using a hymn tune.

Occasions may arise for which the church musician will find it to his advantage to be able to write or arrange a composition for church use. Seasonal and other festivals, dedications, and commemorations are examples. It may be desirable to set a given text or tune for a special service, for which that text or tune may not be available in an arrangement for the group performing it.

If a certain text is desirable, and an appropriate tune is not available, the composer may write an original tune and use it strophically to write an original hymn anthem.

The resources at the composer's disposal, as well as the singers' abilities, must be taken into account. It is obviously unwise to write music which is too difficult for the group which will perform it. It is better to err on simplicity's side. Simple music is many times more effective than complex, difficult music.

CHORAL MUSIC

A strong tune with melodic interest will yield better results than a dull one. Melodies with stepwise motion and skips are better than those with many repeated notes. Repeated notes tend to be dull and to shift the responsibility for interest onto the harmony.

The great tune "St. Anne" has only one repeated note—the sixth note of the first phrase. With this one exception the whole tune moves stepwise or by skips. The tune "Merrial" generally sung to "Now the day is over," is a model of dullness. Of the twenty-four notes thirteen are on E! Chorales, French psalter tunes, and early English hymn tunes are a good source of many strong melodies.

A study of early American tunes will also yield a wealth of interesting material.

The form of the composition as a whole should be determined before beginning to write. Some sort of sketch indicating changes in tonality and modulations and the role of the accompaniment, including introduction, interludes, and final material should be made. It has been my experience with students of composition that if a clear sense of the form of the composition does not exist before the writing begins the piece generally wanders and rambles with no sense of direction. The elements of contrast and climax may be missing or misplaced.

When one has decided to write a hymn anthem and has chosen the tune he may face the temptation to start work with a mere re-harmonization of the tune. After this is done, the question may arise, "What shall I do next?" It is much better to begin work with a sketch of the entire piece.

If there will be an accompaniment, it should be planned in relation to the choral parts. It should give interest and contrast to the piece, not be just a copy of the voices.

From a perusal of hymn-anthem literature it would appear that many accompaniments are almost an afterthought. Many times the introduction is exactly like the opening choral parts, and during the choral sections the accompaniment merely duplicates the voice parts. An independent accompaniment, planned ahead of time and in conjunction with the voices, would likely give a greater sense of unity to the piece and would be more interesting.

Here are some suggestions for writing a hymn anthem, the form for which will be quite simple. The strophic use of the tune somewhat limits the form, and a contrasting change of key may not be practical.

An example of a simple form is: organ introduction; first stanza in unison; interlude; second stanza in two-, three-, or four-part harmony; interlude; third stanza in unison with a descant; and possibly a coda for voices and organ or organ alone.

The voice parts may be extremely simple. The first stanza in unison presents no problem. The second stanza, for variety, may be written in parts, the number and distribution of parts being determined by the resources and ability of the choir. Soprano and alto, or first soprano, second soprano, and alto may be used for women's choirs and proficient junior choirs. With the mixed choir, the usual arrangement is either soprano, alto, tenor, and bass; or soprano, alto, and baritone, depending on the proportion of men available.

This harmonized stanza should be carefully written with strict attention to the rules of voice-leading according to traditional harmony. The inner voices should be interesting and logical, with some motion and an avoidance of many repeated notes. If one has facility in incorporating contemporary sounds into the harmonization, so much the better, but a coloristic device is never an adequate substitute for good craftsmanship. This stanza may be written to be sung unaccompanied.

The third stanza may be in unison with a descant, which is an original melody written above the given tune and which is intended for the sopranos. Descants with phrases which do not end concurrently with the phrases of the hymn tune are generally more interesting than those which do. Care should be taken to avoid parallel fifths and octaves between the melody, the descant, and the bass part of the accompaniment. It is well to remember that the descant is not heard very well if it goes below the melody, and it does not need to be continuous throughout the stanza.

To conclude the composition, there may be a series of "Amens," one elaborate "Amen," a repetition of the last phrase or two, or an original coda for organ based on part of the tune. For some pieces no coda is necessary; for others only a few chords on the organ will suffice.

Writing the chorus parts should present no difficulty. They may be quite easy; in fact, choirs sing easier music more effectively than music which is too difficult for them.

The organ accompaniment makes certain demands on the arranger. It should be written idiomatically for the organ. This means that the composer will compose at the organ, or if he is sufficiently proficient to work at a desk, he will at least play the finished composition on the organ to check for errors. The above suggestions apply also to accompaniments written for the piano.

The introduction should set the mood for the piece and may use thematic material from the hymn tune. This material need not be used exactly as it appears in the tune, but may be modified by changing some of the melodic intervals or the time values of the notes. It should be interesting and should not sound like an introduction to a congregational hymn.

The following excerpt (Figure 50) from Beethoven's Ninth Symphony (sung to "Joyful, joyful, we adore Thee") shows how he modified and expanded a short motif of four notes (measure 1). The second measure contains a passing note. Measures 3 and 4 show additional passing notes and are extended into a cadence.

There need be no complete cadence before the voices enter. In fact, it would probably sound better to lead the accompaniment directly into the voice parts from the dominant or some other chord without settling down on the tonic first.

The accompaniment for the various stanzas should be varied. An accompaniment independent of the voices is the most effective and the most difficult to write. In this type, the accompaniment does not contain the hymn tune but is freely composed to add interest to the composition. The pedal part, and in fact the entire organ part, need not be used continuously. Shorter or extended rests may be used during the choral writing. Detached chords are sometimes effective.

During the harmonized stanza the accompaniment may be much simpler, even following the voice parts themselves. If this stanza is written for treble voices, a bass part, possibly on the manuals with no pedals, is needed to complete the harmony. If written for SAB or SATB, the lowest voice on the organ should be the same as the baritone or bass choral part. Occasionally in SAB writing it

FIGURE 50

may be necessary to give the real bass part to the organ if the baritones have a non-bass note (such as the fifth or seventh of the chord) which, if it were treated as the bass, would violate a rule of harmony or would be difficult or impossible to resolve.

For the final stanza—the voices taking the melody and descant—the accompaniment may be written with the melody on the pedals, the descant in the top voice, and free composition between the two. This helps reinforce the two choral lines. When the hymn tune becomes the bass part, however, chord progressions and the inversions should conform with the rules of classical harmony.

If the composer decides to write a completely original composition it is of prime importance that he make a sketch first.

Tonality and tonal changes should be included in the sketch. First, the key or tonal center should be established. There are sev-

eral ways to do this. An obvious way is to start on the tonic, go to the dominant, and then return to the tonic. Or to start on the dominant, go to the tonic, back to the dominant, and then again to the tonic. These progressions will probably occupy several measures of the composition and need not be the only chords used. Other chords will receive less attention and will occupy less time. Rather, the basic feeling over several measures will be a strong dominant and tonic relationship.

An example illustrating the establishment of a tonal center and the attendant harmonic rhythm is found in the chorus "How lovely is Thy dwelling place" from *A German Requiem* by Johannes Brahms. The first choral phrase extends from measure 4 through measure 13, despite the two commas in the English translation: "How lovely is Thy dwelling place, O Lord of hosts, O Lord of

FIGURE 51

hosts." The chorus begins on the tonic, and the whole first choral phrase (measures 4-13) has a tonic feeling. Other chords within the phrase serve as passing chords. (Figure 51.)

After the tonality has been established emphasis at some other tonal point may be made. In the composer's sketch provision should be made for tonal contrast. Let us imagine a simple A-B-A′ form. Let us say that the basic tonality will be C major for the A and A′ parts of the composition. Section B, for variety, can be in one of the closely related keys: F and G major, and A, D, and E minor. For greater contrast the keys next further removed can be used: D and B flat major, and G and B minor. Actually, any other tonal center can be used as well.

The composer writing in a contemporary idiom may not wish to have a clear-cut classical tonality (a major or minor key, as such). He may wish to establish merely a feeling of a tonal center. A change of tonal center may need to be further removed from the original one in order to produce the needed contrast than is necessary in classical harmony.

Another way to give contrast in contemporary writing is to change the style. For instance, if A is angular, dissonant, and without a strong sense of tonality, the B section can be more consonant and more tonal, possibly with modal coloring.

In part writing of any sort, whether it be the descant, two- or three-part treble, or three- or four-part mixed, all voices should be interesting. Test this by playing each voice through by itself as a melody. Are there many repeated notes? Is there a series of two- or three-note patterns? If so, the part is probably dull. Or is each voice a melody?

The rule of keeping common notes between chords in the same voice is useful only at the beginning of a study of harmony; later on it becomes very dull. In trying to avoid dullness, however, there should not be too many skips. Awkward skips are difficult to sing. Each part should be a melody when played independently and should follow the rules of good voice-leading with the other parts.

From the catalogue of Abingdon Press I have chosen eleven hymn anthems which show in a variety of ways what can be done to create interesting pieces using a pre-existing tune. We will study and analyze each of these anthems and try to discover what the various composers have done and what techniques they have used in their music.

The sixteenth-century chorale "Erhalt uns, Herr" is used by John Dressler in his setting "Lord, Open Thou My Heart." (See page 51.) The four-measure introduction is polyphonic and is based on the first phrase of the tune. The theme (first phrase of the chorale) is given out in the soprano register. The second entrance, on the third beat, at the octave, and in the tenor register, also takes the first phrase of the chorale. The bass part on the pedals begins at measure 2, a fourth below the tenor entrance, and is derived from the theme. The alto voice starts two beats after the bass, an octave higher, and is also derived from the theme. The four voices lead to the dominant at measure 4 and then back to the tonic at measure 5 with the choral entrance.

This introduction shows clearly how thematic material can be used polyphonically. The soprano and the tenor take the first phrase of the tune without alteration. The bass begins the tune, a passing note is inserted (measure 2, beat 4), augmentation is used in measure 3, and the incompleted theme ends on measure 4. The alto imitates the bass (with the inserted passing note) and after the first note the imitation is in augmentation.

For the first stanza the voices take the melody in unison. Against the melody is set a free, flowing accompaniment, with all of its four lines interesting.

The organ interlude following the first stanza (measure 15) is polyphonic and is derived from the first phrase of the melody. The soprano voice takes the complete phrase on the third degree of the scale. The bass takes the whole phrase except the final note at the original pitch. The tenor begins by imitating the soprano but becomes free after the third note.

This leads into the second stanza, at the change of key (measure 18) without a modulation. No modulation, as such, is necessary because the two keys E minor and B minor are closely related, adjacent on the circle of fifths.

This second stanza is interesting for several reasons. The accompaniment is free but the tune appears in one voice or another most of the time. The accompaniment moves; there are no dead spots. Care must be taken not to let the rhythm die on long, final notes of phrases. Look at the accompaniment on the last word of the first phrase, "heart" (measures 20 and 21), and the third phrase, "bless" (measures 26 and 27). The accompaniment moves up scalewise and gives a sense of direction.

The second stanza ends on the B major chord, and the interlude that follows (measures 30-32) begins and ends on the same

chord, the harmonic form of the dominant of E minor, the final key. In the interlude the tonality (because of the C naturals) is drawn back to E minor where it settles at the beginning of the third stanza. The $\frac{6}{4}$ measure (measure 32) before the third stanza uses the ascending melodic E minor scale (C sharp and D sharp). This and the E major triad on the third quarter beat give a feeling of brightness and of anticipation for the next choral entrance.

The first two phrases of the third stanza are repeated in alternation between the men and the women, each group singing in perfect fifths, a coloristic device. The phrases overlap, with the next phrase beginning on the last note of the preceding one. The final two phrases are set in four-part harmony with the melody, somewhat altered, in the alto part.

The accompaniment reinforces the voices by taking their notes and creates a rhythmic drive by the addition of the independent eighth note figures.

On the last syllable of the third stanza (measure 46) the E major triad is used. More somber minor chords follow before the E major triad appears again at the end. In the minor mode, if one wishes to inflect the final chord to major, it is often desirable to introduce that major chord a few measures from the end, as is done in this piece. To do this gives greater strength to the final major chord and does not cause a shock as it might otherwise do.

The modal color in this anthem is quite interesting. The tune itself has the raised seventh degree of the scale (D sharp, the next to the last note of the tune) and the natural seventh degree (D natural, the fourth note of

Lord, Open Thou My Heart

General Anthem for SATB Voices

JOHANNES OLEARIUS, 1671
Tr. Mathias Loy, 1880

JOHN DRESSLER
tune: "Erhalt uns, Herr"
Geistliche Lieder, Wittenberg, 1543

me Thy child and heir re-main.

Sopranos

Thy Word doth deep-ly move the heart,_____ Thy

Word doth per-fect health im-part,_____ Thy Word my soul with

Tenor and Bass

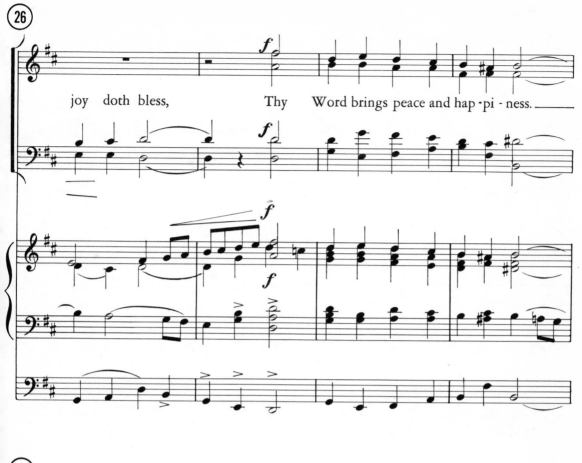

joy doth bless,   Thy   Word brings peace and hap -pi - ness.____

41 (Full Soprano)

Shall glo-ry, praise, and hon-or be Now and_ through-

One, Shall glo-ry, praise, and hon-or be Now and through-

45

out e-ter-ni-ty._____ A - men.

out e-ter-ni-ty._____ A - men.

Ped. *pp*

the first phrase). The raised seventh appears in the harmonic and in the ascending form of the melodic minor scales; the natural seventh is found in the natural or primitive minor and in the descending form of the melodic minor scales. Both the D sharp and the D natural are used freely in the accompaniment. This permits quite a range of E minor as well as G major color which the composer knows how to use.

Then, too, in the second stanza, the B minor section, the use of the C natural as well as the usual C sharp tends to create an ambiguity of modality. The C natural gives a Phrygian color, the C sharp a natural minor color.

The third stanza, with its open fifths and octaves, tends to have a bell-like quality.

"Immortal, Invisible" by Ellen Jane Lorenz (page 57) is an excellent hymn anthem which shows very clearly some of the salient elements of composition which have been discussed earlier.

In Dressler's anthem, just analyzed, we have seen how he used thematic material from the tune itself for the introduction and the interlude after the first stanza. Miss Lorenz illustrates a different kind of writing. She began with original material which can only vaguely be associated with the hymn tune "Joanna" and then only in retrospect. The piece *develops,* as it were, into the familiar recognizable harmonic form at the "Andante" (measure 54), with which, except for a short six-measure coda reminiscent of the beginning, the composition ends.

The opening section of nineteen measures

follows an A-A'-B-A'' form. It is interesting to compare this form with that of the hymn tune which is A-A-B-A'. The first A (measures 1 to 6) shows the simple harmonic progression in F minor: I, IV, I, each two measures long. A' (measures 6 to 10), shortened by two measures, is only four measures long and contains the same basic harmonic progression: I, IV, I, with III (which has the function of V) inserted before the final I.

Now look at A'' (measures 15 to 19), a five-measure phrase. Again the harmonic progression is the same, I, IV, I, but this time the chords are more complex. Seventh chords are used. At measures 16 and 17 the chord is really II_7 (which has a IV function), measure 18 is I_7, and measure 19 is V_7 of E flat major. This last chord is a modulatory one and leads into the next section.

These three A parts of the first section show how phrases can be repeated with enough variation to keep them from being dull and not so much as to make them unrecognizable.

The B phrase (measures 11-14) contains the B phrase of the hymn tune with slight rhythmic alteration. The harmonies in this phrase are varied, too, but lead back to I, by way of the dominant (C major, measure 14), into the A'' phrase.

The second section begins at the "Andantino" (measure 19) and uses the hymn tune in its entirety but not on the original degree of the scale. The tune itself begins on the first degree of the scale. Here it begins on the dominant. The two phrases (A-A) are harmonized with a B flat pedal point. The B phrase of the tune begins on the third degree of the scale instead of the first, permitting the harmony to go to the G minor chord,

Immortal, Invisible

Hymn-Anthem for S.A.T.B. voices

*Tune: "Joanna" (Welsh)

WALTER C. SMITH, 1824-1908

ELLEN JANE LORENZ

*Note: From an amorphous opening ("Hid from our eyes") the Welsh tune gradually evolves.

bless - ed, most glo-rious, the An-cient of Days, Al - might-y,

bless - ed, most glo-rious, the An-cient of Days, Al - might-y,

bless - ed, most glo-rious, the An-cient of Days, Al - might-y,

bless - ed, most glo-rious, the An-cient of Days, Al - might-y,

vic - to - rious, Thy great Name we _ praise. To all, life Thou

vic - to - rious, Thy great Name we _ praise.

vic - to - rious, Thy great Name we praise.

vic - to - rious, Thy great Name we praise.

giv-est, to both great and small,

In all life Thou liv-est, the

Thy wis-dom so bound-less, Thy mer-cy so free, E-

Thy wis-dom so bound-less, Thy mer-cy so free, E-

true life of all; Thy wis-dom so bound-less, Thy mer-cy so free, E-

Thy wis-dom so bound-less, Thy mer-cy so free, E-

ter-nal Thy good-ness, for naught chang-eth Thee. Un - rest-ing,

ter-nal Thy good-ness, for naught chang-eth Thee. Un - rest-ing,

ter-nal Thy good-ness, for naught chang-eth Thee. Un - rest-ing,

ter-nal Thy good-ness, for naught chang-eth Thee. Un - rest-ing,

un-chang-ing, si - lent — as light, Nor want-ing, nor wast-ing, Thou

un-chang-ing, si - lent — as light, Nor want-ing, nor wast-ing, Thou

un-chang-ing, si - lent — as light, Nor want-ing, nor wast-ing, Thou

un-chang-ing, si - lent — as light, Nor want-ing, nor wast-ing, Thou

and the final phrase (A′), begins on the sixth degree of the scale instead of the third. One interval is changed in the last phrase; the interval between the syllables "ness" and "for" (measure 33) is changed from a fourth to a third. The stanza ends on VI with a raised third in E flat major. This is also V in the following F minor section.

At "Tempo primo" (measure 36) there is a repetition of the first section: A (six measures), A′ (four measures), B (four measures), and A″ (five measures) with the same basic harmonies. The repetition is very much like the first statement, but with two important changes: The rhythm is altered in the choral parts due to different textual accents, and the B section, though the basic harmonies are the same, omits the hymn-tune melody except on the words "soaring above" (measures 48 and 49).

The section ends (measure 54) in F minor instead of on the B flat seventh chord because the following section is in A flat major. The F minor chord is VI in A flat major and no modulatory chord is necessary.

Beginning at the "Andante" (measure 54) the hymn tune is set in a traditionally recognizable form with some augmentation at the end. The coda (measure 73) of six measures on F minor reminds one of the beginning and brings the piece to its conclusion in the same tonality with which it began. A piece need not necessarily end in the same tonality it began with, but in this case its doing so gives greater unity to the whole.

George Lynn, in "The Coventry Carol" (page 65) captured the mood of the lullaby. The music shows ingenuity with an economy of materials, and the harmonies are warm and somewhat unusual.

The introductory first four measures, which consist of only two different notes, set the mood. At measure 5 the bass starts the carol melody, and at measure 6 the alto takes the same melody as a canon one octave above. This canon continues for two phrases, a strict canon except for the last note. During this time the soprano and the tenor fill out the harmonies by using the opening two notes with a few others added, thus maintaining the mood set at the beginning.

On the third beat of measure 12 the tenor begins the third phrase of the carol tune and is followed one measure later with the soprano in canon at the octave. This is strict except when, on the first beat of measure 15, the tenor delays moving to the note A until the second beat to avoid parallel octaves with the soprano. The soprano melody is heard as a melody more easily than the inner-voice tenor. Thus one voice needs to be changed, and it is

FIGURE 52

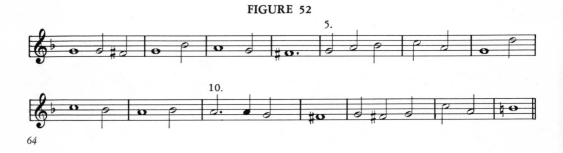

Coventry Carol

S. A. T. B.

(To the George Lynn Singers)

English c. 1591

Paraphrased by
GEORGE LYNN

more logical for the tenor to be changed.

Notice, too, at the last beat of measure 14 in the bass part the four-note descending scale passage. This is thematic material from the tune (Figure 52, notes 5-8, the last beat of measure 7 to the first note of measure 9, and the last beat of measure 9 to measure 11). Was its use as such purposeful or accidental? In this connection the first three notes of the piece are an inversion of the second, third, and fourth notes of the tune. Accidental? I do not know. But it is just such apparently unimportant touches which can give a piece, even a short four-page lullaby such as this, unity and style.

Back to the anthem, at measure 22 the soprano takes the tune and is supported by the three lower voices which move exclusively stepwise except for two intervals, thus continuing the calm, quiet mood of the piece.

The warm rich harmonies and the dissonance evolve from a traditional tonal framework. The dissonance is logical, not contrived. The simple stepwise movement of the voices contributes a great deal to this particular style.

"The Royal Banners Forward Go" by Richard Peek (page 70) shows a very clear A-B-A′ form. The accompaniment is a complete composition independent of the voices. The A sections, in E minor, are identical except for the endings; the first one modulates to A minor, the key of the middle section, and the second remains in E minor and contains a short coda of five measures. Two rhythmic toccata figures are used, one appearing in measure 2, the other in measure 6. The A

section is built around these two motifs, which are interrupted from time to time to insert a harmonized phrase of the plainchant tune.

The B section (measures 29-41), in A minor, is a harmonized version of the tune against a four-note descending scale pattern in the bass. At the conclusion of the tune there is a four-measure bridge into the A′ section.

Three stanzas of the tune are set for unison voices, which double the line of the tune where it appears in the organ part. In the A section each phrase ends with a melismatic extension.

Modal color is used within a traditional tonal setting. The use of the B flat and B natural give a change of color. Successive triads not strictly within a tonality produce contemporary touches. This is seen clearly in measures 66 and 67. The triads are D flat, G, and A major; E flat minor; and C, D, and E major.

This anthem shows how a well-rounded structural form can be built with a minimal amount of musical material—a plainchant tune and two characteristic motifs.

"God of Might, We Praise Thy Name" by Lloyd Pfautsch (page 79) shows still another way to develop a tune.

The second stanza (measure 20) is canonic, though not a strict canon. The imitative voice begins after one measure, one octave below the tune. At measure 22 the imitation stops, but begins again at measure 23 and continues through the phrase. After a repetition of these two phrases the fifth phrase (measure 28) is

the royal banners forward go *

Unison Anthem for Palm Sunday, Lent, or Holy Week

To Elaine Brown

Venantius Fortunatus, 569

RICHARD PEEK

*Based on the plainsong "Vexilla Regis." An organ version of this composition by the same composer is published by The World Library of Sacred Music in the collection *Six Organ Processionals for Coming Into Church.* Permission to use it in the present version is gratefully acknowledged.

The cross shines forth in mys - tic

glow

Where he, as man, who gave man breath,

neath the yoke of death.

Alto and Tenor (Ten. sung at written pitch)

Ful-fill'd is all that Da - vid told

In true pro-phet - ic song of old; How God the na-tions' King

*On a three-manual organ the left hand should be played upon the choir with some 8' Reed tone.

should be,   For God   is reign - ing from the tree.

To thee, e - ter - nal Three in

One,   One,

Let hom-age   meet   by all   be   done:

As

by the cross thou dost re-store.

So rule and guide us ev - er - more.

*If the organ pedal division includes a true 32′ play the right foot an octave higher.

not imitated at all in the lower voice. The imitation is resumed in the final phrase (measure 31) with only one note changed.

The third stanza (measure 41) does not use the tune but is clothed in an original, rich harmonic fabric comprising parallel successions of triads around a D pedal. Additional distinctive color is gained by the use of cross relationship, if not in adjacent triads, at least within the same phrase. F natural, F sharp, C natural, and C sharp are the notes involved. In the last two phrases the pedal moves up to E with the triads above it moved up correspondingly (measures 52-55).

This section does not have a distinct, traditionally tonal sound. There seems to be an attraction to the note D, possibly because it is used as a pedal point. The D major chord, the last chord of the first phrase, sounds more like a dominant than like a tonic, however.

This whole section, beginning at the $\frac{3}{2}$ time signature (measure 33) and ending at "Majestically," avoids any distinct tonal feeling. The attention is drawn to individual notes rather than to keys. The first five measures of this section punctuate the note G and the right-hand chords built up on fourths help to blur the feeling for G major. Beginning with measure 38 in the left-hand part A is forced upon one's attention, with E serving as its dominant. This A in turn becomes a dominant for D at the entrance of the voices. After four phrases on D (10 measures) E becomes the predominant note (measure 54).

In the interlude that follows the conclusion of the voice parts (measure 56), after continuing the E for two measures, there is a shift back to D. This D is retained for the remainder of the organ interlude and becomes

the dominant for G major, the tonality for the last section (measure 64).

This section that we have been discussing is a fine example of a way to gain variety tonally within a piece. In "The Royal Banners" the middle section changes keys, from E minor to A minor and then back to E minor again. In Pfautsch's anthem an A-A-B-A form is used. The A sections are in G major, and in the B section the distinct feeling of tonality is lost. In its place there is an emphasis on individual notes with the superimposed coloristic harmony.

The chorale tune is used again for the final stanza, this time with a descant for the sopranos. The descant phrases overlap with those of the tune; that is, they do not end concurrently with the tune. This makes for more interesting writing, with the attendant rhythmic movement at the ends of the phrases, than there would be if the descant phrase always ended with that of the tune. The descant continues in this fashion until the last phrase (measure 74), where it is discontinued in favor of four-part writing. Two "Amens" end the piece.

The accompaniment contains other interesting features in addition to the ones mentioned in connection with the discussion of the B section. The four-measure introduction at the beginning of the anthem consists of the first five notes of the first phrase and the entire second phrase of the chorale. The top voice of measure 2 is a repetition of measure 1, but it is one diatonic step higher.

The rhythm for the first stanza accompaniment is established at measure 5 and remains constant until the final phrase. This rhythm gives contrast to that of the tune. The freely

God of Might, We Praise Thy Name

(Grosser Gott, wir loben dich)

S.A.T.B. Hymn—Anthem

Attr. to Ignaz Franz, 1719-1790
Trans. J. H. Horstmann, 1908, alt.*

Katholisches Gesangbuch, Vienna c. 1774
Arr. Lloyd Pfautsch

*With permission of Eden Publishing House.

Look u - pon Thy chil-dren here who, to Thee their love pro -

Look u - pon Thy chil-dren here who, to Thee their love pro -

Look u - pon Thy chil-dren here who, to Thee their love pro -

O Lord_____, O Lord_____,

p (optional)

composed interlude which follows leads into and dovetails with the following unaccompanied stanza.

The next interlude changes to $\frac{3}{2}$ which has as many quarter notes per measure as $\frac{6}{4}$ but has the accents occurring at different places in the measure. In $\frac{6}{4}$ meter the accents are on the first and fourth quarter notes. In $\frac{3}{2}$ meter they occur on the first, third, and fifth quarter notes. At the end of this interlude there is a change to duple meter: $\frac{4}{2}$ and occasionally $\frac{2}{2}$.

On the last stanza, beginning at "Majestically," the right hand of the accompaniment is written in $\frac{3}{2}$ meter, with all the other parts in $\frac{6}{4}$. This means that two meters are being used at the same time. This continues until near the end.

At measure 76 the bass of the accompaniment is the same as measure 1 at the beginning of the piece. Measure 77 continues the quarter note rhythm.

This anthem shows how thematic material can be developed and how original material can be introduced to good advantage.

"Arise, My Soul, Arise!" by Dale Wood (page 86) is of a much more simple construction than the preceding one.

The tune, a Finnish folk melody, is a simple A-B-A-B-C-B-A'-B. Because of the amount of repetition (three A's and four B's) in the tune itself, there is no need to develop it, and too, folk tunes many times sound best in simpler settings.

The tune is used twice, the first time in unison. The second time the men begin (measure 38) and the women enter a measure later and imitate the pitch of the first six notes with two rhythmic changes. The women's phrase is shortened, and the phrase is ended in octaves. The next phrase is in octaves. These two phrases are repeated. Then for sixteen measures the melody is harmonized in four parts, and the rhythm is augmented to twice the preceding values. The last two phrases are in octaves with the last three notes harmonized.

It is interesting to note that the four-measure organ introduction is derived from the C part of the tune. Of the eight parts of the tune, C occurs only once. It is logical for this C to be used because it will be heard the least number of times. The pitches of C are used, the first half in measures 1 and 2. From the last beat of measure 2 to measure 4 the tune is put a third lower than it appears originally. The fanfare rhythm of the introduction is different from that of the tune. This introduction is used as the accompaniment beginning with measure 21 (with the original C of the tune in the voice part).

There is an interesting succession of major triads beginning at measure 2: E, D, C, B flat, C, D (with an added sixth), and E. Such a succession of all major triads creates brightness and contrasts the Dorian melody which follows.

At the end of measure 9 there is an organ phrase which is again derived from C of the tune. This variant is used as an interlude between the two stanzas (measures 36-38) and again at measure 76.

The accompaniment enters one measure after the voices begin (measure 5) and takes the same melody as a canon at unison pitch.

Arise, My Soul, Arise!

General Anthem for SATB Voices

JOHAN KAHL, 1721-46
Tr. ERNEST RYDEN, 1886-

FINNISH FOLK MELODY
Arr. DALE WOOD

Text used by permission of the Commission on the Liturgy and Hymnal, authorized by the Lutheran Churches co-operating in the Commission on the Liturgy and Hymnal.

worship Him in hum-ble-ness and own Him Lord. His_
ban-quet of love A - waits thee a-bove; Be-
hold, the mar-riage fes-tal of the Lamb is come! Re-
joice, my soul, re-joice, To heav'n lift up thy

Reeds

Gt.

never-end-ing an-them sound-ing through the sky. To

To mor-tals is not given, its
mor-tals is not given To chant its strains all glo-rious; Yet

p (*senza rit.*)

sing, my soul, the praise of Him who reigns on high. Who

(voices alone)

55 bought with His Blood The ran - somed of God;

62 To Him be ev - er - last - ing pow'r and vic - to -

69 ry. ___ And let the great A - men Re - sound through heav'n a -

74 gain. Al - le - lu - ia, Al - le - lu - ia, Al - le - lu - ia!

How Firm A Foundation

Anthem For S. A. B. Choir

"K" In RIPPON'S Selection
1787

Early American Melody
Arr: Samuel Walter

31

still give thee aid; I'll strength-en thee, help thee and cause thee to

aid; I'll strength-en thee, help thee and cause thee to stand, Up -

36

stand, Up - held by my right-eous om - ni - po-tent hand.

held by my right-eous om - ni - po-tent hand.

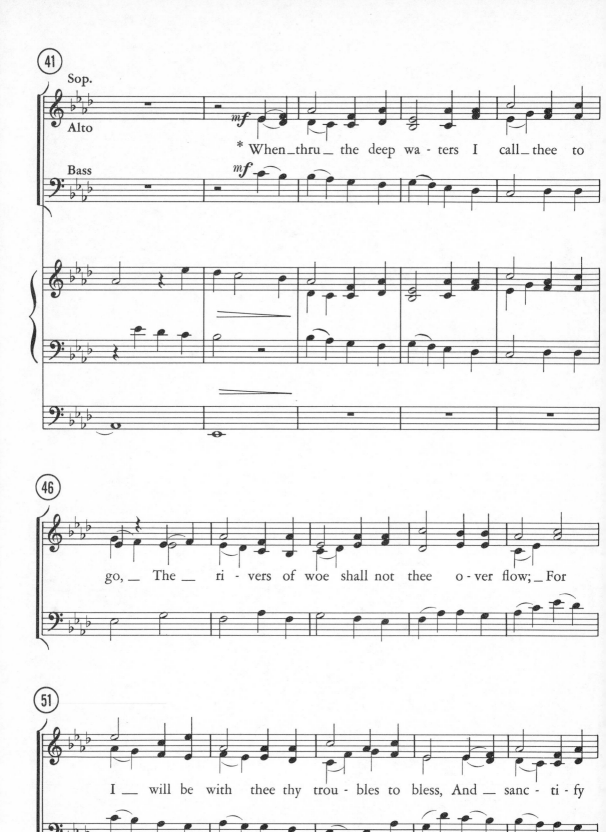

to __ thee thy deep - est dis - tress.

Sop.

ff

Alto

The __ soul that on Je - sus still leans for re -

Bar.

ff

Ritard.

a tempo

mf

a tempo

mf

shake,

I'll __ nev - er, no, nev - er, no nev - er, for -

sake.

ritard.

Fragments of the tune appear in the accompaniment from measure 26 to measure 32.

Beginning with the second stanza of the voices (measure 38) the accompaniment takes the first two phrases of the tune in augmentation which is extended to the section in four-part harmony (measure 54).

When the accompaniment again enters (measure 71), fragments of the tune are used to the end of the piece.

Again unity and interest are achieved by the simplest of means, thematic material for the accompaniment being derived from the folk tune.

My own "How Firm a Foundation" (page 91), based on an early American melody, was written with the idea of keeping the voices rather simple and the melody clearly heard.

The first stanza is in unison, the second is a strict canon, and the third is harmonized for soprano, alto, and baritone. The last stanza begins with the soprano and baritone taking the melody and the alto taking a simple consonant part. Beginning with "That soul" (measure 70), the baritone starts the phrase and the alto and soprano, in turn, enter in imitation for the entire phrase. The organ trumpet also imitates the phrase with three added notes. The last phrase is two parts—melody and descant. The organ imitates this last phrase two measures later (measure 78), but with some alteration.

The very simple organ introduction contains the beginning of the tune in the left hand and the end of the tune in the right.

The accompaniment for the first stanza is a simple harmonization of the tune. The interlude which follows contains a triadal fragment from the tune. During the strict canon of the voices in stanza 2 the organ has an original canon which leads into the unaccompanied third stanza. The fourths in the right hand of the interlude which follows again make use of the triadal fragment and lead into the final stanza with its independent accompaniment.

"Easter Bell Carol" by Lloyd Pfautsch (page 99) is unusual because it is for unison voices and handbells. The voice part is an A-A-B-A form with a short coda at the end.

The thematic material of the four-measure introduction is used throughout. Measure 3, with its eighth notes, is used at the end of each A section (measures 12 and 48). The accompaniment is the same for all the A sections, and the introduction is repeated before the final A. The accompaniment is well written for handbells, and the anthem is a fine illustration of how a very simple accompaniment can be added to a melody to produce a delightful composition.

My "Christ Is the World's True Light" (page 104) was written for a definite purpose. My rector, the Reverend Stanley F. Hemsley, had heard this hymn, liked it, and wanted to introduce it to the congregation. He suggested that the choir use it as an anthem. To ask the choir to sing it from the hymnal did not appeal to me, so I arranged it as a hymn anthem.

For Dr. F. Lee Whittlesey and his choirs
Highland Park Methodist Church, Dallas, Texas

Easter Bell Carol

For Handbell and Unison Choirs

LLOYD PFAUTSCH

LLOYD PFAUTSCH
Arr. from a 12th century
German melody

57741

God in Christ is glo - rious. He has been vic -

to - rious! Lift now your voice to __ sing: Hal - le -

lu - - - jah! Hal - le - lu - jah!

Hal - le - lu - jah! Hal - le - lu - jah! _____

ritard.

poco rit.

I was anxious to keep the tune unchanged so that it would be more easily learned by the congregation when their turn came to sing it as a hymn.

The first stanza in my arrangement is just unison. Or rather it is in octaves because the men sing an octave below the women. The second stanza is harmonized and is intended to be sung unaccompanied. It was originally written for SATB. I reharmonized it for SAB before submitting it for publication because I thought it would be more useful in the latter form.

Writing three-part harmony is in some ways more difficult than writing in four parts. In this unaccompanied version the baritone is the real bass. If it is kept as the true bass it may at times be impossible to have all three tones of a given triad. This occurs when the melody has the same note (or octave) as the baritone. As a result the texture sounds thin, but it is preferable to keep the baritone as a real bass rather than permit it to become a harmonic voice.

I tried to give contrast to this thin three-part texture by using some unison (or octave) writing. The third phrase is in octaves until the last note, and the fourth and final phrases end on octaves.

The third stanza is simply the melody with an optional descant. The descant phrases end one measure after those of the melody, except for the last one which is shortened to end with the melody. I decided that since the descant lies quite high, those performing should sing it on the syllable "Ah." If a text were given the vowels (except "Ah") would need to be modified anyway toward the "Ah" sound because of the high register; also, two simultaneous sets of words would not be understood by a congregation. This would have been the case if words had been given to the one-measure-removed descant phrases.

After one measure of accompaniment the final phrase is repeated, harmonized, as a coda. The text is appropriate for repetition.

This tune, "St. Joan," is somewhat unusual in that it contains several phrases which are only three measures long instead of the customary four measures. The length of the phrases (number of measures) is 3, 4, 3, 4, 3, 3, 3, 3.

The introduction of the accompaniment opens with the first phrase of the melody. Measure 4 begins a four-measure phrase of free material which overlaps the voice parts by one measure. After a rest of three beats, the independent accompaniment continues, written in a thin three-part texture which thickens to four or more parts at the end of the four-measure phrases.

At measure 20 the accompaniment anticipates the following phrase by one measure and is played an octave higher. Actually the voice part becomes a canonic voice. The canon is abandoned after two phrases in favor of a simple chordal accompaniment contrasting the voice part. The interlude which follows the first stanza is freely composed and is not based on the hymn tune.

The interlude following stanza 2 (measure 61) makes use of the first and last phrases of the hymn tune, with one note changed. In the last stanza the accompaniment reinforces the melody and the descant, the left hand (with the pedals) takes the melody, and the top voice has the descant with an occasional altered note.

FIGURE 53

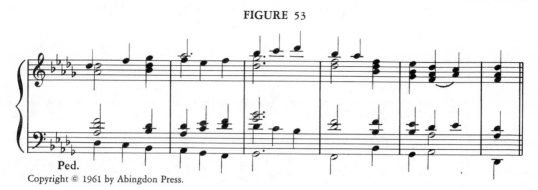

Ped.

The accompaniment was originally written for organ. From the second measure of the introduction to the entry of the voice part, for instance, the left hand was originally assigned a chord instead of a single note an octave above the pedals. (See Figure 53.) When this composition was being prepared for publication, the editor suggested that I revise the accompaniment to make possible its performance on the piano.

The voice parts are easy, and the composition would have greater usefulness if it could be performed in churches using a piano. I readily agreed to make the necessary changes. The accompaniment for the first stanza did not need to be rewritten because it was already written for manuals alone. For the remainder of the anthem the left hand was placed within an octave of the pedals.

Originally in the last stanza the left hand took chords similar to those in the right hand. Doubling the melody (on the pedals) an octave higher was substituted for these chords. What was lost in harmonic texture was made up in greater reinforcement of the melody.

Sometimes one encounters the reverse of what we have been discussing—a piano accompaniment which will be modified to permit adequate performance on the organ. In this case the bass part should not go below C, the second added line below the F clef. This C is the lowest note on the organ pedalboard. Consecutive chords with a span of an octave (for one hand) should be avoided unless a detached style is desirable; it is difficult to play such chords legato on the organ. Typical pianistic devices used with the damper pedal, such as arpeggios or successions of the same chord in different octaves or positions, may sound awkward or frivolous on the organ and may need to be changed. Only if the lowest voice is a true bass part should it be assigned to the organ pedals. Even so, it can be a relief and a contrast to omit the organ pedals at times.[1]

The scansion of the poem "Christ Is the World's True Light" reveals an irregular rhythm; the lines begin with either a strong or a weak syllable, and the rhythm of one stanza differs from that of another. The accents of the music are regular; the primary accent is on the first beat of the $\frac{3}{4}$ meter. Oc-

[1] Figure 3, pp. 20-23 of my book, *Basic Principles of Service Playing* (Nashville: Abingdon Press, 1963), shows several examples of pianistic writing and how they can be modified for the organ. Even though these examples are intended for performance, they are useful for composers as well because they show some idiomatic differences between the two instruments.

To the Rev. Stanley F. Hemsley, rector of St. John's Episcopal Church, Stamford, Conn.

Christ Is the World's True Light

Hymn-Anthem for SAB Voices

GEORGE WALLACE BRIGGS

Arr. Samuel Walter
based on the Hymn Tune "St. Joan"
by PERCY E. B. COLLER

Christ is the world's true Light, Its Cap-tain of Sal-va - tion,

The Day-star clear and bright— Of ev-'ry man and na - tion;

New life, new hope a-wakes, Wher-e'er men own his sway: Free-dom her

28 bond - age breaks; And night is turned to day.

35 Soprano
Alto *mf* In Christ all ra - ces meet, Their an-cient feuds for-get - ting,
Baritone

43 The whole round world com - plete____, From sun - rise to__ its set -

49 ting: When Christ is throned as Lord, Men shall for - sake their

55 fear, To plough-share beat the sword, To pru - ning - hook__ the
To_____ beat__ the sword,

Ped.

casionally the textual accent falls on the second beat of the measure instead of the first. The textual accent differs from that of the music. This, however, does not alter the basic meaning of the text. This shift in accent may occur in syncopated passages. An example of this is found in the anthem "Glo-*ry* to God *in* the high-*est*" by Giovanni Pergolesi.

Sometimes a normally unaccented, final syllable will be accented, as in the following, well-known chorales:

> Now thank we all our God
> With heart and hands and voic-*es*.

> A mighty fortress is our God
> A bulwark never fail-*ing*.

If a poem is set to a metrical tune occasional discrepancies may occur between the basic word and music accents. If the composer sets a text to original music, however, he should, in general, give more emphasis to strong textual accents than to weak ones, by placing these accents on strong beats of the music, on notes of longer duration, or notes of a higher pitch.

"O Thou Eternal Christ, Ride On!" by Austin C. Lovelace (page 109) is very simple in construction and easy to analyze. The tune, "Llangloffan," is a variant of the familiar A-B-A form: A-A'-B-A'. After a unison first stanza, the second one is harmonized in four parts. The A sections are all harmonized slightly differently. This gives variety to the setting. A glance back to "Christ Is the World's True Light" will show the same type of varied harmonies for phrases using the same

melody (stanza 2, phrases 1, 3, and 7—measures 36-38, 43-45, and 56-58).

The third stanza of Lovelace's anthem is unison and descant for the A sections and unison or two parts for the B. The mode is changed from minor to major in keeping with the brighter inflection of the text.

The descant is not continuous. The melody begins alone, and the descant, when it enters, gives rhythmic accent to the tune but without obscuring it. The descant disappears in the B section and is heard once again for the final phrase.

Of interest is the repetition of the note D throughout this last stanza. D is emphasized in the descant of the A sections and in the accompaniment of the B section. At measure 56 the D reappears. D is the dominant note, and both this and the tonic notes and triads are important in this piece.

The introduction makes use of the A' part of the tune; it appears in augmentation at measure 3 and overlaps the voice part.

The accompaniment contains the melody in its top voice for the A sections and is free in the B part. Note the sequence in measure 20. The top voice of the accompaniment is derived from the voice part of the preceding measure. Notice, too, the repetition of this material in the interlude following the unaccompanied stanza (measures 38 and 39).

It is interesting to see a return of the augmentation (in measures 3-5) at the very end of the composition ("Voices in Unison" line at measure 55).

The accompaniment adapts itself well to either the organ or the piano. It stays within the range of the organ and contains no idiomatic idiosyncrasies.

O Thou Eternal Christ, Ride On!

S. A. T. B.

*CALVIN W. LAUFER, (1874-1938)

"Llangloffan"
Arr. AUSTIN C. LOVELACE

O Thou E-ter-nal Christ of God, Ride on! Ride on! Ride on! Es-tab-lish Thou for ev-er-more The tri-umph now be-gun. A might-y host, by Thee re-deemed, Is march-ing in Thy train: Thine

go with Thee to claim and build A cit-y un-to God.

39

Soprano Descant

a tempo **f**

Ride on!

Voices in Unison **f** *a tempo*

O Thou who art the Life and Light, Ex-

cresc. e rit. **f** *a tempo*

44

Lord and King, Ride on! Ho-

alt-ed Lord and King, We hail Thine au-gust maj-es-ty And

48

san - nas sing! Un - til in ev - ery

Soprano-Alto

loud ho - san - nas sing, Un - til in ev - ery

51

maestoso
ff

land and clime Thine ends of love are won:

ff *maestoso*

land and clime Thine ends of love are won: O·

54

poco rit.

Christ, Re - deem - er, __ Broth - er, Friend, Ride on! Ride on! Ride on!

poco rit.

poco rit.

Carol of the Advent

Advent or Christmas Anthem for SATB voices

Besançon Carol Tune
Arranged by PHILIP DIETTERICH

ELEANOR FARJEON

Text from The Oxford Book of Carols. Used by permission of Oxford University Press.

glad. Though earth is bare, one more seed is plant-ed there: Give up your

strength the seed to nour-ish, that_ in course the flow-er may flour-ish. Peo-ple, look

East, and sing to-day: Love, the rose, is on_ the way.

(Sop.)

(Alto) Birds, though ye long have ceased to build,

(Ten.)

(Bass)

(Voices unaccompanied)

night is dim _____ one more light the bowl _ shall brim, shin-ing be -

dim one more light the bowl _ shall brim, shin-ing be-yond the fros - ty

yond the fros - ty weath-er, bright _ as sun _ and moon _ to - geth - er. Peo-ple, look

weath-er, bright as sun _ and moon _ to-geth - er. Peo-ple, look East, and sing to -

East, and sing to - day __ : Love, the star, is on _ the way.

day: Love, the star, is on _ the way _____ .

Philip R. Dietterich uses a Besançon carol tune in his "Carol of the Advent" (page 113). After a chord giving the tonality the first stanza is sung by the sopranos unaccompanied. Single-line unaccompanied music can be very effective and is in keeping with the tradition of the church. Unison plainchant, the backbone of church music, has been sung for many centuries without accompaniment, and where it is sung today many of its admirers maintain that plainchant retains its pristine beauty to the fullest extent only when it is performed without accompaniment. I might add that I share this view.

The Protestant churches of today could make much more use of unaccompanied unison singing. I do not mean men and women singing in octaves, just unison by men *or* women. With this unison singing the listeners can give their full attention to the melody, unencumbered by harmony, pleasing though the latter may be.

Stanza 2 (measure 17) is for men in unison. In stanza 4 (measure 47) the men take the melody and the women a canonic voice. It is an example in which a strict canon is not used. It begins three eighth notes after the melody and an octave above, but later (the middle of measure 50) it is a measure away. Measures 53 and 54 contain free imitation, and the canon is continued an octave and a third above the melody in measure 54. Beginning with "People, look East" (in measure 56), the interval is an octave again, but here the canon is not strict.

A canon need not be strict. Notes here and there can be modified to suit the harmonies.

Imitation need not be continued throughout the stanza though in this case it is. The composer's imagination will determine to what extent strict or free imitation will be used.

The last stanza is in octaves except the last four measures. The melody can begin at the beginning of the measure as it does here or on the fourth eighth note as it does at the beginning of the composition. The four-part harmony in the last line expands the last phrase of the melody from two measures to four but not by the usual augmentation of each note. Measure 72 is derived from the tune, but the intervals are different. Measure 73 can be considered a sequential treatment of measure 72, and the remainder of the melody starts on the high A flat in measure 73.

The third stanza (measure 33) has not thus far been mentioned because it consists of original music. This stanza creates as great a contrast as is possible with the other parts of the anthem; the melody is new; the tempo is slower (a quarter equals the preceding dotted quarter); the meter is changed from $\frac{6}{8}$ to $\frac{4}{4}$; there is a change of key and mode (from E flat major to C minor); instead of unison voices with accompaniment, unaccompanied harmonies are used; and the mood is more somber.

The accompaniment is simple in keeping with the nature of the carol. The interlude following the unaccompanied first stanza (measure 15) is derived from the melody and in the stanza that follows, the accompaniment contains the melody most of the way either at the pitch of the voices or an octave above them. The next interlude (measure 30) is the last phrase of the tune. The interlude after the original stanza (second half of measure 45) makes use of the first five notes at the beginning of the carol. The fourth note is higher than the third, though the interval is not the same as that of the carol. These five notes are repeated as a sequence at a high pitch before leading into the voice parts.

The accompaniment for the canonic stanza (measure 47) is unobtrusive, sometimes taking snatches of the melody and sometimes not, so as not to obscure the melody and the canonic imitation. The final stanza is more sustained and is written for the organ.

Orchestral instruments are being used in the church with increasing frequency, and church musicians should have some knowledge about them. Choral literature written with orchestral accompaniment sounds best when performed as originally intended. This includes music of Bach, Handel, Mendelssohn, Mozart, Schubert, Brahms, and others. Most churches, however, cannot afford to hire the entire orchestra specified by the composer. As a compromise, the use of a few judiciously chosen instruments will give additional aesthetic value to the performance. The vocal solos of Bach, for example, consist, many times, of the vocal line, an instrumental melody, and a simple accompaniment for strings or continuo.[1] The solo instrumental voice is often as important musically as the voice line, and whenever possible the instrument should be used. The organist should omit the solo instrumental part from the accompaniment and play only the continuo or an arrangement of the string parts.

WRITING FOR OTHER INSTRUMENTS

The following are examples of works that can be performed with organ and a few instruments: Fauré's *Requiem*—harp, violin, and optional horns in F; Brahms' *Requiem*—tympani, violin, and optional harp; Handel's "The trumpet shall sound" from *The Messiah* —trumpet (trumpet in D, if possible); and Schubert's *Mass in G*—string quartet.

These instrumental parts are generally available from publishers, but in some cases they

[1] "Continuo. In the scores of Baroque composers (Bach, Handel), the bass part which was performed by the harpsichord or organ, together with a viola da gamba or cello." Willi Apel, *Harvard Dictionary of Music* (Cambridge, Mass.; Harvard University Press, 1953), pp. 182-83.

may need to be copied from the orchestral score. Copyrighted works require the permission of the owner of the copyright if parts are to be copied. Care must be taken in copying parts to make sure that the notes, rests, accidentals, changes of key and time signature, and dynamics are correct.

The following sign is used to show consecutive measures of rests: ⊢⁸⊣ means that there are eight measures of rests. A change of meter within these measures of rest must be indicated. Figure 54 means that there are

FIGURE 54

three measures of rests, the rhythm changes to ¾, and then there are four measures of rests.

At services for which additional instruments are used it may be desirable to have these instruments play the prelude, offertory, postlude, and hymns with or without the organ. These pieces may require some arranging to make them playable.

Instruments can take a stanza of a hymn without the organ. Accompaniment by a hand-bell choir is effective. If amateur instrumentalists are used they should not be expected to play continuously on all stanzas of a hymn. Woodwind and brass players may need to rest their lips. For this reason, and for variety, the organ alone can take alternate stanzas.

The arranger should be acquainted with the range of the instruments at his disposal. Figure 55 is a chart showing the range of best tones and the actual sounds of the more common instruments. The use of the saxophone, marimba, xylophone, and vibraharp in church

is questionable, since these instruments remind one of popular music.

Four clefs are used by the instruments. The familiar G, or soprano, clef places G above middle C on the second line of the staff. The F, or bass, clef places F below middle C on the fourth line. The C clef is movable and is used to indicate middle C. It is generally used on the third line, alto clef, and on the fourth line, tenor clef.

The B flat clarinet, B flat trumpet, and horn in F are transposing instruments. The printed note C, when played on a B flat instrument, will sound B flat, a whole tone below it. Therefore music transcribed for B flat instruments from music using concert pitch (choral and organ music) must be transposed up one whole tone. Music transcribed for horn in F must be transposed a perfect fifth up.

Figure 56 shows the first two measures of "St. Anne" transcribed for string quartet, woodwind quartet, and brass quartet. In the second version, for both strings and woodwinds, the parts are rearranged in a higher octave to give more brilliance. If the organ is used, the clarinet, oboe, and flute can all take the melody and the bassoon the bass, with the organ filling out the harmonies. In the string quartet both violins can take the melody, the first violin playing the melody an octave above the second violin (the latter taking the original pitch of the melody). Single instruments, particularly those capable of playing in higher registers, should take the melody.

The composer with one or more instruments at his disposal may wish to transcribe pieces or write original compositions for them. The hymn-tune prelude is an excellent form

FIGURE 55

Normal Range of Instruments

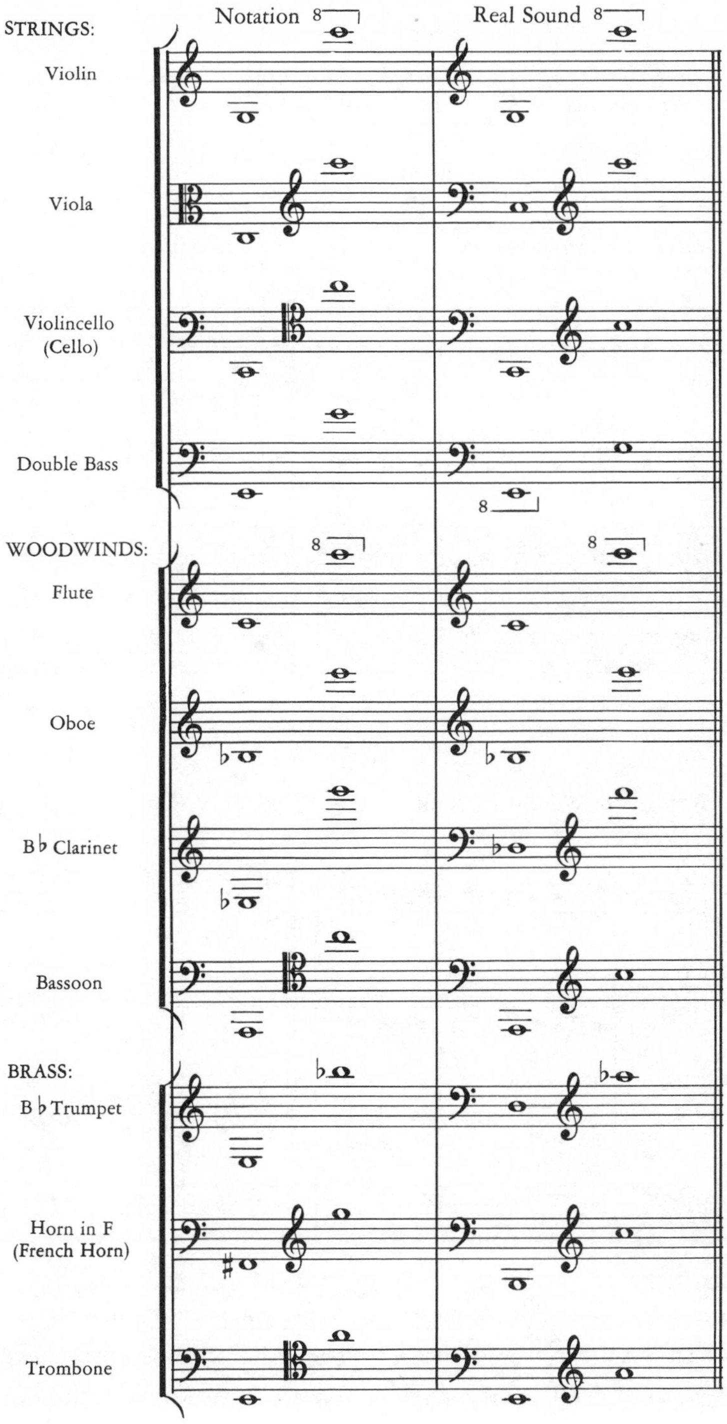

St. Anne

to use. This form is easily adapted to one instrument with organ or to several instruments with or without organ. If one instrument will be used it can play the melody, with the organ taking the polyphonic and harmonic voices. The melody should be placed in the best register of the instrument playing it, so that the instrument will be heard to best ad-

FIGURE 56

Arranged for Brass Quartet (2 B♭ trumpets, 2 trombones)

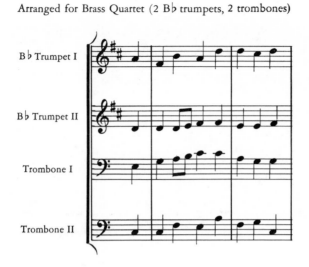

Arranged for Brass Quartet (1 B♭ trumpet, 2 horns in F, 1 trombone)

vantage. The composition may be written with the melody in any register, even the bass, or an octave above normal soprano range if this suits the instrument. The violin and flute sound fine in this high register, and the cello, the bassoon, and the trombone, while they sometimes take a bass part, can take the melody in the tenor register.

Two or more blending instruments may be used antiphonally with the organ: orchestral strings and organ flutes, brass with organ principals and mixtures up to full organ, and woodwinds with appropriate contrasting organ color.

With the use of the collection, *Nine Compositions for Organ,* I shall show how these pieces can be arranged for one or more instruments.

In the prelude "O Gott, du frommer Gott" the melody is in the top voice and can be played by violin, viola, oboe, clarinet, or trumpet, with the organ taking the lower two voices. The prelude can be arranged for three instruments, such as violin, viola, and cello. If a second violin is available the two violins can play the melody in octaves. If a double bass takes the lowest voice the D sharp in measure 8 is below its range. This D sharp and the E preceding and succeeding it should be written an octave higher. If only the D sharp was written an octave higher there would be two awkward skips of a seventh. By the same token from measure 24 to the first beat of measure 33 the double bass part should be written an octave higher. The C clef on the third line should be used for the viola part.

The combination of one or two trumpets on the melody and two trombones for the lower voices would be effective. If these instruments are used the piece will need to be transposed up to be in the range of the trombones—D minor for trombones and E minor for B flat trumpets. This might sound rather shrill. A whole tone down (C minor for the trombones and D minor for the B flat trumpets) would probably sound better, but in this case, the second trombone part, from the last beat of measure 28 through the first beat of measure 33, should be written an octave higher to bring the part within the trombone's range.

Similarly, a combination of woodwinds, such as oboe, clarinet, and bassoon, can be used if the piece is transposed up to bring it within their range. The middle voice, which goes down to one octave below middle C, exceeds the range of oboe and clarinet. The horn in F can be used for the middle voice with either brass or woodwinds.

"Kirken den er et" presents several interesting possibilities. If only one instrument is available it may play the bass melody or the top voice canon, whichever lies in the range of the instrument, with the organ taking the remaining parts. If there are two instruments of possible range both the melody and the canon can be taken by them. The prelude has no more than four voices at any one time, making it possible to use four instruments of appropriate range. If the piece is transcribed for a string quartet, for example, the top line will be for the first violin, the second line for the second violin, the third line for viola, and the lowest (the pedal part) for cello. This works consistently except at measure 37. The B flat is beyond the viola's range. Here the viola will rest while the cello takes that part for measure 37 and the first note of measure 38. The viola will begin playing again on the last note of measure 38.

"Eucharistic Hymn" lends itself well to an arrangement for string quartet and organ. It may be transcribed as follows.

The organ takes the first seven measures and the first beat of measure 8. The strings enter on the first beat of measure 8, overlapping the organ, taking the harmonized version of the hymn tune, to the first beat of measure 24. The organ pedals begin at measure 23 and the manuals at measure 24. (See Figure 57.) The organ continues through measure 27 for the second harmonized setting of the hymn tune. The top voice (Violin I) drops out at the end of measure 43, the second voice (Violin II) at the end of measure 44, the third voice (Viola) after the first beat of measure 44, and the lowest voice (Cello) at the end of measure 42. The organ begins in the pedals at measure 43, the left hand on the second

FIGURE 57

measures 23-25

beat of measure 44, and the right hand at measure 45. The organ can finish the composition, or the strings may enter at measure 49 and both the organ and the strings continue to the conclusion. If this is done the cello need not take the bass line but can take one of the manual voices. The left hand "Solo ad lib." beginning on the last beat of measure 52 would sound fine as a cello solo. This solo should then be omitted from the organ part.

"Rendez à Dieu" is an example of a piece which can easily be arranged for one instrument and organ. An instrument sounding best in the tenor register should be used, for example, cello, bassoon, trombone, or horn in F. There is no time signature in the original. A time signature should be written into the solo instrumental part. Figure 58, written in the C clef on the fourth line for cello, bassoon, or trombone, shows the notation for

FIGURE 58

the first phrase. The solo part ends on measure 35.

The melody of "Herzliebster Jesu" is set twice, both times in the soprano register. The first time it is in the pedal part with a four-foot flute which brings the sound up to the soprano. This melody would sound fine for violin, viola, oboe, clarinet, and possibly trumpet. If intended for B flat clarinet or B flat trumpet, the part should be transposed to A minor. The solo part should conclude at the end of measure 41 with only the organ finishing. The organ part should omit the melody taken by the solo instrument.

The melody of "Liebster Jesu" can be taken by violin, viola, oboe, or clarinet. A flute or violin could take the melody an octave higher than written. If this is done it might be a good idea to rewrite the organ part by giving the right hand the same notes as the left. (See Figure 59.)

If six brass instruments are available, for example, three trumpets and three trombones, or other combinations including horns in F, they can be used in place of the organ reeds in "Hyfrydol." The fanfarelike interludes contain six parts except at measures 40 and 41. Here the lowest note of the four-note chords in the right-hand part should be omitted. Beginning with measure 79 both the organ and brass can finish the piece, the brass taking simple F triads beginning at measure 81 (Figure 60), with the organ playing all the notes as written. The sign used in the second measure of Figure 60 means that the preceding measure is to be repeated.

FIGURE 59

FIGURE 60

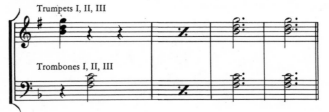

In the toccata "Slane" the melody is used twice. Any combination of brass instruments would be fine for the melody. Trombone should start on middle C and continue one octave above the written melody. The melody begins at measure 3 in the pedal part. The trumpet part should be written to sound at the same pitch as the trombone (D above middle C for the B flat trumpet). At measure 23, even though the melody is in a high soprano register and a proficient trumpeter would be able to play it, the brass can be written in the same register as it was the first time. Beginning with the last beat of measure 41, freely composed parts which harmonize with the original music and are in a good range for the instruments can be written.

"God rest you merry" does not lend itself, to my mind, to instrumental adaptation. Part of the interest in a theme and variations for organ lies in the variety of colors possible on the instrument. Introducing other instruments would not greatly add to the colors available, and this particular piece is idiomatically best suited to the keyboard instrument.

Handbells are becoming increasingly popular in churches throughout the country, and the director of the handbell choir should know how to arrange music for it.

Helen M. Runkle, who organized "The Bell Ringers of Cape Ann" (Gloucester, Massachusetts) in 1938, has supplied the following information and has given me permission to use it and to quote from her arrangements.

Mrs. Runkle's Bell Ringers have given concerts throughout New England, including a concert at Boston's Museum of Fine Arts in 1960, and in Washington in 1956, on the occasion of President Eisenhower's lighting the national community Christmas tree. She began by using only eight bells. Gradually she added six more.

The pitches of a set of fourteen bells is shown in Figure 61. Although sharps are always used to designate bells of chromatic pitches, the enharmonic equivalent is also used in notation. B flat is regularly used in the key of F.

With fourteen bells the following keys are available: C, F, G, and D major; A and E, natural minor; and D and B, natural and harmonic minor.

The larger and more popular twenty-five bell set consists of two complete chromatic octaves and one note, from G below middle C to two octaves above. With this set all keys are available, and the arrangements can be more interesting and varied than with smaller sets. Larger sets are available, up to the sixty-one bell, five chromatic octave set.

In arrangements for bells a thin texture is better than a thick one. Figure 62 shows examples of several kinds of arranging: single-line melody with occasional chords (*a*), two-part writing (*b*), chordal writing (*c*), or a combination of these (*b* and *d*), both of which are from the same arrangement.

Inversions may be freely used except on the

FIGURE 61

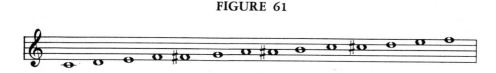

FIGURE 62

a. O Come, O Come, Emmanuel   ANCIENT CHANT

b. Cradle Song of the Infant Jesus   FRENCH CAROL

c. Silent Night   FRANZ GRÜBER, 1787-1863

d. Cradle Song of the Infant Jesus   FRENCH CAROL

swing

Used by permission of J. Fischer & Bro., Glen Rock, N.J., from *A Handbell Concert,* by Helen M. Runkle.

final chord, which should be in root position. For smaller sets of bells a full four-part chord in root position may not be possible, for example, in the key of G on a fourteen bell set. Here one can end on the tonic note G alone.

The melody may be in the top, inner, or lowest voice. Single-line melodies with occasional chords to show harmonic changes are effective. Pedal point may be used.

Possibly the best and easiest type of writing is the theme and variations, working from very simple, single-line melodies to complex, rhythmic, and varied settings.

Many churches own both a piano and an organ, and if they are in tune with each other as they should be they may be used together.

The piano, a percussion instrument, has its own idiosyncratic idiom and is used a great deal for secular music; hence the use of the piano in church may be questioned. It may be difficult to make the piano sound sacred.

If the church has both an organ and a piano, however, the piano is probably intended to be used other than as a substitute instrument when the organ breaks down.

If both instruments are to be used for congregational singing the standard organ technique and a suitable adaptation for the piano are all that is necessary. Appropriate ways for playing hymns on the piano in church are dealt with at length in William S. Mathis' book, *The Pianist and Church Music.*[2]

[2] Nashville: Abingdon Press, 1962.

In arranging from orchestral scores, if a harp is not available, that part may be played on the piano. The harp tones die quickly; the harp does not have the fullness of tone of the piano. The piano will sound more like a harp if the soft pedal is used, causing the hammers to strike only one string per note instead of the usual three, and thus reducing the piano's normal fullness of sound. If a grand piano is used the music rack should be removed, the entire lid closed, and the soft pedal used. The music rack may be placed on top of the lid for reading the music. Played according to these instructions, some grand pianos make good imitation harps. The damper pedal may be used sparingly and should be released about two seconds after the note is played or, for fast arpeggios, after each group of notes. Because of the divergence of tone and the variety of ways of writing for the harp, it is difficult to give more explicit directions on the use of the damper pedal. The pianist should listen carefully and experiment with various techniques until he gets the best sounds possible for the particular piano he is playing.

Examples of orchestral works, the harp part of which may be played on the piano, include Brahms' and Fauré's *Requiems.*

Occasionally the celesta is used. The celesta is a keyboard instrument which sounds similar to the harp. Music for celesta may be played on the piano. The soft pedal should be used, but not the damper pedal, and the notes should be played one octave higher than they are written. Honegger uses the celesta in his *King David.*

Most church musicians are more or less acquainted with piano technique. Any typically pianistic device, as long as it is in good taste and appropriate for church use, may be used. The composer may wish to write some solo piano pieces for performance in church. It is suggested that he read the chapter on "Writing for Organ," and then compose according to his imagination and in keeping with the idiom of the piano.

Duets for piano and organ may be written. Both instruments need not be used constantly. Either one may have extended solo passages because each instrument is complete in itself.

When both instruments are playing, if the organ has the melody, the piano can take a pianistic figure, such as the arpeggio, to give contrast and rhythmic vitality. Or the piano may take the melody with the organ accompanying it appropriately.

The melody for the piano need not be only in single notes; it may be played in octaves, three notes in octaves, or both hands in octaves, depending on the sonority desired. It is possible for the piano to take a melody and also to have some accompanimental notes, but it might be best to keep the texture rather thin so that all the notes of both instruments can be heard.

For toccatas and other very loud pieces care must be taken to see that the organ will not drown out the piano. Arpeggios and other toccata figures (see Figures 38-47) on the organ do not sound nearly as loud as do sustained chords. Heavy chordal writing for the piano and fast-note figures for the organ will probably give better balance and permit the piano to be heard adequately.

AFTERWORD

One should not be discouraged with his first attempts at composition. Only with practice can the skill be developed. On the other hand, one should not feel that one's first efforts are great works of art; they probably are not. Only after years of study and application can the craft be perfected. Even then, relatively few compositions show real imagination and originality. Early compositions may fill a need for particular situations, however, or they may arise from the creative urge of the composer. If one or both of these reasons for writing should be the composition's only merit, composing is still a worthwhile endeavor.

Atkisson, Harold F. *Basic Counterpoint.* New York: McGraw-Hill, 1956.

Boyden, D. *A Manual of Counterpoint Based on Sixteenth Century Practice.* Rev. ed. New York: Carl Fischer, Inc., 1953.

Bush, Alan D. *Strict Counterpoint in Palestrina Style.* London: Joseph Williams, Ltd., 1948.

LIST OF RECOMMENDED BOOKS

Dallin, L. *Techniques of Twentieth Century Composition.* Dubuque, Iowa: William C. Brown Company, 1958.

Mathis, William S. *The Pianist and Church Music.* Nashville: Abingdon Press, 1962.

Parry, Scott B. *The Story of Handbells.* Boston: Whittemore Associates, Inc., 1957.

Persichetti, Vincent. *Twentieth Century Harmony.* New York: W. W. Norton & Company, Inc., 1961.

Piston, Walter. *Counterpoint.* New York: W. W. Norton & Company, Inc., 1947.

———. *Harmony.* Rev. ed. New York: W. W. Norton & Company, Inc., 1962.

Tapper, Thomas. *First Year Harmony (Augmented and Newly Revised Edition).* Evanston, Ill.: Summy-Birchard Company, 1959.

Trobian, Helen R. *The Instrumental Ensemble in the Church.* Nashville: Abingdon Press, 1963.

Tufts, Nancy Poore. *The Art of Handbell Ringing.* Nashville: Abingdon Press, 1961.

INDEX

NOTES